The Art of Body Piercing: Mastering the Techniques and Building a Successful Career

Imprint:
Eder Sebastian
Obere Hofmark 8
84543 Winhöring
sebastiansbuecher@gmail.com

1.
Introduction

Welcome to the captivating world of body piercing! In this introductory chapter, we embark on a journey to explore the art, history, and significance of body piercing. From ancient traditions to modern expressions of individuality, we uncover the rich tapestry that surrounds this unique form of body modification.

We begin by delving into the historical roots of body piercing, tracing its origins back to ancient civilizations. From ancient Egypt and Rome to tribal cultures across the globe, we discover the various cultural and spiritual meanings attached to piercing throughout history. We explore how body piercing has evolved over time, from a symbol of status and ritualistic practice to a mainstream form of self-expression.

Next, we dive into the different types of body piercings, highlighting the vast array of options available to individuals today. From earlobe piercings to facial, body, and even intimate piercings, we explore the diverse range of placements and jewelry choices that cater to personal style and individuality. We discuss the significance and cultural associations tied to each type of piercing, allowing readers to gain a deeper understanding of the artistry behind these modifications.

As we explore the world of body piercing, we also emphasize the importance of safety and hygiene. We discuss the role of professional piercers and the essential steps they take to ensure a safe and sterile piercing environment. From the use of sterile equipment to thorough aftercare instructions, we provide readers with valuable insights on how to approach body piercing with caution and responsibility.

Furthermore, we delve into the emotional and psychological aspects of body piercing. We examine the motivations behind individuals seeking piercings, whether it be for self-expression, personal empowerment, or a desire to connect with a particular subculture. We also address the common misconceptions and stigmas surrounding body piercing, emphasizing the importance of respect and acceptance for individual choices.

Throughout this book, our aim is to provide readers with a comprehensive guide to body piercing. From understanding different piercing techniques to navigating the aftercare process, we equip readers with the knowledge and resources necessary to make informed decisions about their piercing journey.

So, whether you're a piercing enthusiast, considering your first piercing, or simply intrigued by the world of body modification, join us on this enlightening adventure. Together, let's unravel the mysteries and celebrate the beauty of body piercing in all its forms.

Furthermore, in this comprehensive guide to body piercing, we delve into the fascinating realm of piercing techniques and procedures. We explore the intricacies of each technique, from traditional needle piercing to advanced methods like surface anchors, industrial piercing, and frenulum piercing. Readers will gain a deeper understanding of the intricacies involved in these techniques, including placement, healing process, and potential risks.

As we navigate through the world of body piercing, we also address the importance of sterilization and infection prevention. We delve into the rigorous sterilization protocols followed by professional piercers, ensuring a safe and hygienic environment for clients. By understanding the sterilization processes and tools used, readers will develop an appreciation for the meticulous attention to detail required in the piercing industry.

Moreover, we highlight the significance of client safety and comfort during the piercing process. We discuss the importance of effective communication and consent, ensuring that clients are fully informed and comfortable with their chosen piercing. Additionally, we explore techniques to manage pain and anxiety, providing readers with valuable insights and strategies to enhance the overall piercing experience.

Throughout the book, we emphasize the critical role of aftercare in the healing process. We provide comprehensive instructions for various types of piercings, empowering readers to take proper care of their new adornments. From cleaning techniques to recognizing signs of infection, our aim is to promote healthy healing and minimize complications.

Additionally, we address the potential risks and challenges associated with specific piercing types. By understanding the unique considerations for each piercing, readers will be equipped to make informed decisions and take necessary precautions. We provide insights into potential complications and how to address them effectively, ensuring a smooth and successful piercing journey.

Lastly, we emphasize the importance of ongoing education and professional development for piercers. We delve into the various opportunities available for piercers to expand their knowledge and refine their skills. From attending conferences and workshops to pursuing advanced certifications, readers will discover pathways to elevate their expertise and stay abreast of the latest trends and advancements in the field.

With this comprehensive guide, readers will gain a thorough understanding of the world of body piercing. Whether you're an aspiring piercer, a seasoned professional, or simply curious about the artistry behind body modification, this book serves as a valuable resource to navigate the world of piercing with confidence, knowledge, and creativity.

2.
The History of Body Piercing

Body piercing has a rich and diverse history that spans thousands of years and countless cultures around the world. From ancient rituals to modern fashion statements, the practice of adorning the body with pierced jewelry has evolved and transformed over time.

One of the earliest recorded instances of body piercing dates back to ancient Egypt, where both men and women adorned themselves with various types of piercings. Earrings were particularly popular among the elite, symbolizing wealth and status. Egyptians believed that earrings had magical and protective powers, and they were often buried with their earrings to accompany them into the afterlife.

In ancient Rome, body piercing took on a different significance. Roman soldiers would pierce their nipples as a sign of bravery and to display their loyalty to the empire. This practice later extended to other parts of the body, including the genitals, as a symbol of virility and strength.

Throughout history, body piercing has also played a significant role in cultural and religious rituals. In many indigenous tribes, piercing was seen as a rite of passage, marking the transition from childhood to adulthood. The Maasai tribe of East Africa, for example, practiced earlobe stretching as a sign of beauty and maturity.

In some cultures, body piercings held spiritual and religious significance. Hinduism, for instance, embraces the concept of body piercing as a means of connecting with the divine. Nose piercings, specifically the left nostril, are believed to enhance a woman's fertility and marital happiness.

During the Renaissance period, body piercing fell out of favor in Europe due to its association with paganism and non-Christian practices. However, it experienced a resurgence in the 20th century, influenced by various subcultures and movements such as punk, goth, and the LGBTQ+ community.

In the 1970s and 1980s, body piercing gained mainstream attention, thanks in part to influential figures like Jim Ward and Fakir Musafar, who established piercing studios and pioneered safe and hygienic piercing techniques. This era saw the rise of new piercing trends, including navel piercings, eyebrow piercings, and multiple ear piercings.

Today, body piercing has become a form of self-expression and personal style. It is embraced by people from all walks of life, regardless of age, gender, or social status. From simple earlobe piercings to elaborate full-body adornment, the possibilities are endless.

It is important to note that body piercing should always be done by trained professionals using sterile equipment to minimize the risk of infection and other complications. Following proper aftercare instructions is crucial for ensuring proper healing and maintaining the health of the pierced area.

In conclusion, the history of body piercing is a testament to humanity's enduring desire for self-expression and the importance of cultural and personal identity. From ancient civilizations to modern subcultures, body piercing has left its mark on societies worldwide. It continues to evolve and adapt, reflecting the ever-changing attitudes and values of individuals seeking to express themselves through this timeless art form.

Body piercing has a rich and fascinating history that spans across different cultures and time periods. The practice of piercing the body dates back thousands of years and has served various purposes in different societies.

Ancient civilizations such as the Egyptians, Romans, and Greeks practiced body piercing for religious and cultural reasons. In Egypt, body piercing was associated with royalty and the nobility, with pharaohs and high-ranking individuals adorning themselves with intricate piercings and jewelry. The Romans and Greeks, on the other hand, used body piercings to denote social status and as a form of personal expression.

In certain indigenous tribes and cultures around the world, body piercing was and still is a significant part of rituals and ceremonies. It is believed to symbolize the passage into adulthood, tribal affiliations, or spiritual connections. These piercings often have deep cultural meanings and are passed down through generations.

During the Middle Ages, body piercing fell out of favor in many European societies due to the influence of the church, which viewed it as a form of self-mutilation. However, it continued to be practiced in other parts of the world, particularly in tribal communities.

The resurgence of body piercing in Western culture can be traced back to the 1960s and 1970s when the counterculture movement embraced it as a form of rebellion and self-expression. This marked the beginning of the modern body piercing movement as we know it today.

In the 1980s and 1990s, body piercing gained mainstream popularity and became more widely accepted. This was fueled by the emergence of piercing studios and professional body piercers who emphasized safety, hygiene, and proper techniques. The availability of high-quality piercing jewelry also contributed to its growing popularity.

Today, body piercing has evolved into a thriving industry with a wide range of piercing options and styles. From traditional earlobe piercings to more elaborate and unique placements like septum piercings and surface anchors, individuals have countless options to express their individuality and style.

It's important to note that body piercing is not just a passing trend or fashion statement. It carries cultural significance, personal meaning, and serves as a form of self-expression for many individuals. Understanding the history of body piercing allows us to appreciate its cultural roots and the journey it has taken to become an integral part of contemporary society.

3.
Understanding Different Types of Piercings

Piercings have been a part of various cultures around the world for centuries. They serve as a form of individual self-expression and can represent a multitude of meanings and symbols. To fully understand the world of piercings, it is important to recognize the different types of piercings and explore their unique characteristics.

One widely known and popular piercing is ear piercing. It can be placed in various areas of the ear, including the earlobe, cartilage, and outer ear. Popular variations of ear piercing include tragus piercing, helix piercing, and conch piercing. Each one has its own distinct features and offers individual customization options.

Another common piercing is nose piercing. There are different options available, including nostril piercing, septum piercing, and bridge piercing. Each nose piercing can accentuate facial expression and give the wearer a distinctive look.

Lip piercing is also popular and can be placed in various locations around the mouth. Labret piercing, Monroe piercing, and Medusa piercing are just a few examples of lip piercings, each with its own aesthetic appeal.

For those who want to emphasize their tongue, there is tongue piercing. It can be placed horizontally or vertically and allows the wearer various jewelry options to enhance their individual style.

Navel piercing is also a popular choice, particularly among younger individuals. It is placed in the area of the navel and can be an aesthetically pleasing addition to the body.

Furthermore, there are genital piercings that are placed in the genital area. These include Prince Albert piercing, Christina piercing, and clitoral piercing. These piercings require special care and hygiene as they are placed in sensitive areas of the body.

Each type of piercing has its own unique characteristics and requires specific care and attention during the healing process. It is important to thoroughly research the risks, healing process, and aftercare instructions before getting a piercing.

Understanding Different Types of Piercings provides a comprehensive insight into the variety of piercings available today. It allows readers to explore the different options and discover their own preferences. Whether you're interested in ear piercings, nose piercings, lip piercings, or other types, this guide will help you make informed decisions about your personal style.

In addition to the aforementioned piercings, there are several other types that individuals may consider. One such piercing is the eyebrow piercing, which involves placing jewelry through the eyebrow area. This piercing can create a bold and edgy look, enhancing the facial features.

Cheek piercing is another option that some individuals choose to showcase their unique style. It involves placing jewelry on the cheek, typically on the dimples area. This type of piercing requires careful consideration due to the potential risks involved.

For those looking for a more intricate and elaborate piercing, dermal piercing is an option worth exploring. Dermal piercings involve placing a decorative anchor underneath the skin, allowing for the attachment of various jewelry pieces. This type of piercing can be placed on different areas of the body, such as the chest, back, or face, creating a striking and distinctive appearance.

Nipple piercing is also a popular choice, particularly among individuals seeking to express their individuality and enhance their body aesthetics. It involves placing jewelry through the nipple area, and it can be done on both men and women.

When considering any type of piercing, it is crucial to take into account personal preferences, body anatomy, and potential risks. Consulting with a professional piercer who follows proper safety and hygiene practices is essential to ensure a safe and successful piercing experience.

Understanding Different Types of Piercings not only provides information on the various piercing options available but also emphasizes the importance of proper aftercare. It covers topics such as cleaning routines, potential complications, and signs of infection to help individuals maintain the health and integrity of their piercings.

By gaining a comprehensive understanding of the different types of piercings and their unique attributes, individuals can make well-informed decisions and express their personal style confidently. Whether someone is interested in subtle ear piercings or more adventurous body piercings, this guide serves as a valuable resource to navigate the world of piercings.

4.
Piercing Techniques and Procedures

Piercing is a form of body modification that involves creating an opening in the skin or cartilage to insert jewelry. It is important to understand the various techniques and procedures involved in the piercing process to ensure a safe and successful experience.

The first step in any piercing procedure is proper preparation. This includes sterilizing the equipment, such as needles and forceps, to minimize the risk of infection. The piercer will also cleanse the area to be pierced and mark the exact placement of the piercing to ensure accuracy.

Once the preparation is complete, the piercer will use a sterile needle to create the opening. The needle is carefully inserted into the desired location, and the jewelry is then inserted through the needle. The piercer may use forceps to hold the skin or tissue in place during the procedure to ensure precision and minimize discomfort.

Different types of piercings require different techniques. For example, earlobe piercings are relatively straightforward and can be done with a single needle. On the other hand, more complex piercings, such as the belly button or nipple, may require additional tools or specialized techniques.

The piercing procedure should always be performed by a professional piercer who has received proper training and has experience in the specific type of piercing being performed. This helps ensure the highest level of safety and reduces the risk of complications.

After the piercing is complete, the piercer will provide aftercare instructions to promote proper healing. This may include cleaning the piercing with a saline solution, avoiding excessive touching or twisting of the jewelry, and avoiding certain activities, such as swimming or using certain beauty products, that may irritate the piercing.

It is important for individuals to follow these aftercare instructions closely to minimize the risk of infection and promote healthy healing. Regular check-ups with the piercer may also be recommended to monitor the healing process and address any concerns or issues that may arise.

In addition to the technical aspects of piercing, it is crucial for piercers to prioritize client comfort and safety throughout the entire procedure. This includes creating a clean and welcoming environment, ensuring proper sanitation practices, and effectively communicating with clients to address any questions or concerns they may have.

In recent years, there have been significant advancements in piercing techniques and tools. For example, the use of sterile disposable needles and high-quality jewelry materials has become more prevalent, enhancing safety and reducing the risk of complications. Additionally, the development of advanced piercing techniques, such as surface piercings or dermal anchors, has expanded the range of piercing options available.

In conclusion, understanding the various piercing techniques and procedures is essential for both piercers and individuals interested in getting a piercing. By ensuring proper preparation, using appropriate techniques, and providing comprehensive aftercare instructions, professional piercers can create a positive and safe piercing experience for their clients. Remember, always choose a reputable piercer who prioritizes hygiene, safety, and client satisfaction.

As the field of piercing continues to evolve, it is important for piercers to stay updated with the latest advancements and techniques. Ongoing education and training programs are available for piercers to enhance their skills and expand their knowledge.

One significant development in piercing techniques is the use of numbing agents or topical anesthetics to minimize pain during the procedure. These products, when used correctly and under professional guidance, can help alleviate discomfort and create a more comfortable experience for clients.

Another important aspect of piercing procedures is the consideration of individual anatomy. Every person's body is unique, and piercers must take into account factors such as skin thickness, blood vessels, and nerve endings when performing a piercing. This ensures that the procedure is not only aesthetically pleasing but also safe and comfortable for the client.

In recent years, there has been a growing emphasis on aseptic techniques in piercing procedures. Aseptic technique refers to a set of practices that aim to prevent the introduction of microorganisms and reduce the risk of infection. This includes using sterile equipment, wearing gloves, and maintaining a clean and controlled environment throughout the piercing process.

Additionally, piercers are increasingly adopting a more holistic approach to piercing. This includes considering the emotional and psychological well-being of clients. Piercers may engage in active listening and communication to understand their clients' motivations and expectations for getting a piercing. This allows them to provide personalized recommendations and ensure that clients are fully informed and comfortable with their decision.

Furthermore, the field of piercing is witnessing advancements in jewelry options. There is now a wide range of high-quality materials available, such as surgical-grade stainless steel, titanium, and biocompatible plastics. These materials not only offer aesthetic options but also reduce the risk of adverse reactions or allergies.

It is worth noting that while piercing techniques and procedures have evolved, the fundamental principles of hygiene, safety, and professionalism remain unchanged. Piercers must adhere to strict health and safety regulations, maintain proper sterilization protocols, and prioritize client education and aftercare.

In conclusion, the field of piercing techniques and procedures has experienced significant advancements in recent years. These advancements focus on enhancing client comfort, ensuring safety, and providing a wide range of options for individuals seeking piercings. As piercers continue to adapt to these developments, they contribute to creating a positive and fulfilling experience for their clients.

5.
Sterilization of Tools and Equipment

Sterilization of tools and equipment is a crucial aspect in the field of piercing. It plays a pivotal role in maintaining hygiene and preventing infections during the piercing process. In this chapter, we will delve into various methods and techniques of sterilization to ensure that piercing studios and piercers adhere to the highest standards of safety and cleanliness.

Importance of Sterilization
Sterilization is of paramount importance in the piercing industry as it eliminates harmful microorganisms, including bacteria, viruses, and fungi, from tools and equipment. By ensuring proper sterilization, piercers can significantly reduce the risk of infections and other complications for their clients.

Autoclave Sterilization
One widely used method of sterilization in piercing studios is autoclave sterilization. Autoclaves use high-pressure steam to eliminate microorganisms effectively. We will explore the process of autoclave sterilization in detail, including the proper loading and operation of the autoclave, as well as the maintenance of sterilization indicators.

Chemical Sterilization
Chemical sterilization is another method commonly employed in the piercing industry. It involves using specific chemicals to kill or inhibit the growth of microorganisms on tools and equipment. We will discuss various chemical agents, such as glutaraldehyde and hydrogen peroxide, their effectiveness, and the necessary precautions to ensure safe usage.

Sterile Packaging

Once the tools and equipment have been properly sterilized, it is essential to maintain their sterility until they are ready for use. Sterile packaging techniques, such as using autoclave bags or sterilization pouches, play a crucial role in preserving the sterility of the instruments. We will examine the correct methods of packaging and storing sterilized tools to prevent contamination.

Routine Monitoring and Maintenance

Sterilization equipment and processes require regular monitoring and maintenance to ensure their effectiveness. We will delve into the importance of routine biological and chemical monitoring tests to validate the sterilization process. Additionally, we will explore the significance of equipment maintenance, including regular cleaning and servicing, to uphold the sterility standards.

Compliance with Health and Safety Regulations

Piercing studios must comply with local health and safety regulations regarding sterilization practices. We will provide an overview of the relevant regulations and guidelines to help piercers understand their legal obligations and ensure a safe environment for both themselves and their clients.

In conclusion, the proper sterilization of tools and equipment is crucial in the piercing industry to prevent infections and ensure the safety of clients. By following the appropriate sterilization methods, such as autoclave sterilization and chemical sterilization, and implementing sterile packaging techniques, piercers can maintain high standards of hygiene. Routine monitoring, maintenance, and compliance with health and safety regulations further contribute to creating a safe and sterile environment in piercing studios.

Training and Education
To ensure the effective implementation of sterilization practices, it is essential for piercers to receive proper training and education. This includes understanding the importance of sterilization, learning the correct techniques for sterilization, and staying updated with the latest advancements in sterilization technology. We will discuss the significance of ongoing education and training programs for piercers to enhance their knowledge and skills in maintaining a sterile environment.

Cross-Contamination Prevention
Cross-contamination is a significant concern in piercing studios, as it can lead to the transmission of infections between clients. We will explore strategies to prevent cross-contamination, such as the use of disposable items, dedicated workstations for each client, and strict adherence to hand hygiene practices. By implementing these preventive measures, piercers can further minimize the risk of infections.

Quality Assurance and Documentation
Maintaining a comprehensive record of sterilization processes is vital for quality assurance and accountability. We will discuss the importance of documentation, including recording sterilization cycles, tracking expiration dates of sterilization indicators, and maintaining a log of routine monitoring tests. These practices not only ensure compliance but also enable traceability in case of any incidents or audits.

Sterilization Best Practices
In this section, we will highlight some best practices for sterilization in piercing studios. This includes establishing standardized protocols for cleaning, disinfection, and sterilization, as well as implementing a regular review and update process for these protocols. We will also emphasize the importance of creating a culture of accountability and responsibility among piercers and studio staff regarding sterilization practices.

Client Education
Educating clients about sterilization practices is essential to instill
confidence and trust in the piercing process. We will discuss the
importance of explaining sterilization procedures to clients, addressing
their concerns regarding hygiene and safety, and providing aftercare
instructions to minimize the risk of infections post-piercing.

Emerging Trends in Sterilization
Lastly, we will touch upon emerging trends and advancements in
sterilization technology. This may include innovations in sterilization
equipment, such as advanced autoclaves or sterilization methods
utilizing ultraviolet (UV) light. By staying informed about these trends,
piercers can continuously improve their sterilization practices and
ensure the highest level of safety for their clients.

In conclusion, the sterilization of tools and equipment is a critical
aspect of the piercing process. By following proper sterilization
methods, piercers can maintain a safe and hygienic environment,
minimizing the risk of infections. With ongoing training, adherence to
regulations, and implementation of best practices, piercing studios can
provide a professional and trustworthy experience for their clients.

6.
Infection Prevention and Control Measures

Infection prevention and control are paramount in the field of piercing to ensure the safety and well-being of both clients and piercers. This chapter will explore a range of measures and protocols that are essential in preventing and controlling infections in piercing studios. By implementing these measures, studios can maintain a clean and hygienic environment, reducing the risk of complications and promoting a positive piercing experience.

Hand Hygiene
Hand hygiene is a fundamental practice in infection prevention. Piercers must thoroughly wash their hands with soap and water before and after each client interaction. Alternatively, they can use alcohol-based hand sanitizers with a high percentage of alcohol content. By practicing proper hand hygiene, piercers can minimize the transmission of microorganisms from their hands to the client's piercing site.

Personal Protective Equipment (PPE)
The use of appropriate personal protective equipment is vital to protect both piercers and clients. Piercers should wear disposable gloves during every piercing procedure, ensuring they are changed between clients. Additionally, masks and protective eyewear may be necessary to minimize the risk of airborne contamination. Adhering to proper PPE protocols creates a barrier against potential pathogens and maintains a sterile environment.

Surface Disinfection

Thorough and regular disinfection of surfaces is essential to prevent the spread of infections in piercing studios. All work surfaces, chairs, and equipment should be disinfected before and after each client. The use of EPA-approved disinfectants ensures the efficacy of the cleaning process. Additionally, disposable barriers, such as plastic wraps or disposable sheets, can be used to cover surfaces and minimize the risk of contamination.

Aseptic Technique

The application of aseptic technique during piercing procedures is crucial to prevent infections. This involves maintaining a sterile field by using sterile gloves, sterile single-use needles, and sterile equipment. Strict adherence to aseptic technique reduces the introduction of microorganisms into the piercing site, minimizing the risk of infections and promoting faster healing.

Safe Handling and Disposal of Sharps

Proper handling and disposal of sharps, such as needles and lancets, are essential in preventing injuries and the transmission of bloodborne pathogens. Piercers should use puncture-resistant containers for the disposal of used sharps and ensure they are disposed of in compliance with local regulations. Regular training on safe sharps handling should be provided to all studio staff.

Client Assessment and Screening

Thorough client assessment and screening are crucial steps in infection prevention. Before performing a piercing, piercers should assess the client's medical history, including allergies, immunization status, and any existing health conditions that may increase the risk of complications. Clients should also be screened for signs of infection, such as fever or skin conditions, which may require further evaluation or postponement of the piercing procedure.

Informed Consent and Aftercare Instructions
Obtaining informed consent from clients is an essential part of infection prevention. Piercers should ensure that clients are fully aware of the potential risks and aftercare requirements associated with the piercing procedure. Clear and detailed aftercare instructions should be provided to clients to minimize the risk of infections and promote proper healing.

Bloodborne Pathogen Training
Piercers and studio staff should receive regular training on bloodborne pathogens, including HIV, hepatitis B, and hepatitis C. This training should cover methods of transmission, prevention strategies, and the importance of vaccination. By being knowledgeable about bloodborne pathogens, piercers can implement effective prevention measures and protect themselves and their clients.

Regular Health and Safety Audits
To maintain a safe and hygienic environment, regular health and safety audits should be conducted in piercing studios. These audits ensure compliance with infection control protocols, evaluate the effectiveness of sterilization and disinfection practices, and identify areas for improvement and further training. Audits may include assessing the proper use of PPE, reviewing sterilization logs, and checking the overall cleanliness of the studio. By conducting regular audits, studios can identify any gaps in infection control measures and take corrective actions to enhance safety.

Education and Training
Continuous education and training are vital components of infection prevention and control in piercing studios. Piercers and studio staff should stay updated on the latest techniques, guidelines, and best practices in infection control. This includes attending seminars, workshops, and certification programs related to infection prevention. By investing in education and training, studios can ensure that their staff members have the knowledge and skills necessary to implement effective infection control measures.

Communication and Collaboration

Effective communication and collaboration among piercers, studio staff, and clients are essential in infection prevention. Studios should establish clear lines of communication for reporting any potential infections or concerns. Collaboration with local health authorities and infection control experts can provide valuable guidance and support in maintaining a safe environment. Open and transparent communication fosters a culture of safety and enables prompt action in case of any infection-related issues.

Continuous Improvement

Infection prevention and control measures should be subject to continuous improvement. Studios should regularly review and update their protocols based on new research findings, emerging pathogens, or changes in regulatory requirements. This includes staying updated on industry standards and guidelines set forth by professional organizations. By embracing a culture of continuous improvement, studios can adapt to evolving challenges and provide the highest level of infection prevention and control.

In conclusion, infection prevention and control measures are crucial in piercing studios to ensure the safety and well-being of clients and piercers. By implementing effective hand hygiene practices, using appropriate PPE, maintaining proper surface disinfection, adhering to aseptic techniques, and emphasizing client assessment and education, studios can create a safe and hygienic environment. Regular audits, education and training, collaboration, and a commitment to continuous improvement further enhance infection control efforts.

7.
Client Safety and Comfort during the Piercing Process

Ensuring the safety and comfort of clients during the piercing process is of utmost importance in piercing studios. This chapter will delve into various measures and considerations that are crucial in promoting a safe and comfortable experience for clients. By implementing these practices, piercing studios can establish a positive and trustworthy reputation while prioritizing client well-being.

Client Education
Educating clients about the piercing process is key to their safety and comfort. Prior to the procedure, piercers should provide comprehensive information about the piercing itself, including the risks, aftercare, and potential complications. This empowers clients to make informed decisions and prepares them for what to expect during and after the piercing.

Informed Consent
Obtaining informed consent is a vital aspect of client safety. Piercers should ensure that clients fully understand the procedure, risks, and possible outcomes before proceeding with the piercing. This includes discussing any potential allergic reactions, risks associated with specific body placements, and the importance of following aftercare instructions.

Studio Hygiene
Maintaining a clean and hygienic studio environment is essential for client safety. Piercing studios should adhere to strict sanitation protocols, including regular cleaning and disinfection of work surfaces, equipment, and seating areas. The use of disposable barriers and single-use sterile tools further reduces the risk of cross-contamination.

Sterilization Practices

Thorough sterilization of piercing tools and equipment is crucial to prevent infections. Piercers should follow appropriate sterilization techniques, such as autoclaving or using single-use disposable instruments. Regular monitoring and documentation of sterilization processes ensure that the tools used are free from harmful microorganisms.

Body Placement and Jewelry Selection

Expertise in body placement and jewelry selection is essential for client safety and comfort. Piercers should carefully assess anatomical factors, such as skin type, thickness, and vascular structures, to determine suitable placement options. Additionally, they should guide clients in selecting appropriate jewelry that minimizes the risk of complications and promotes proper healing.

Pain Management

Minimizing client discomfort is a priority during the piercing process. Piercers should employ effective pain management techniques, such as topical anesthetics or cold compresses, to reduce pain and alleviate anxiety. Clear communication with clients about the potential level of pain associated with the specific piercing helps manage their expectations.

Gentle and Precise Technique

Adopting a gentle and precise piercing technique is crucial for client comfort and safety. Piercers should use proper hand positioning, accurate needle placement, and controlled movement to minimize trauma and reduce the risk of excessive bleeding or tissue damage. Ensuring a calm and reassuring environment also helps clients feel more at ease during the procedure.

Aftercare Instructions
Providing clear and detailed aftercare instructions is essential for client safety and successful healing. Piercers should explain proper cleaning techniques, appropriate products to use, and potential signs of infection. Clear communication and written instructions help clients understand how to care for their new piercing and prevent complications.

Ongoing Support and Follow-up
Offering ongoing support and follow-up care demonstrates a commitment to client safety. Piercers should be readily available to answer questions, address concerns, and provide guidance throughout the healing process. This includes scheduled check-ups to assess the healing progress and ensure client satisfaction.

Continuous Professional Development
Engaging in continuous professional development is essential for maintaining client safety and comfort. Piercers should stay updated on the latest industry advancements, techniques, and safety practices through seminars, workshops, and networking with fellow professionals. By expanding their knowledge and skills, piercers can provide a higher level of care and address client needs more effectively.

Client Feedback and Satisfaction
Listening to client feedback and prioritizing their satisfaction contributes to ongoing improvement in client safety and comfort. Piercers should actively seek feedback from clients regarding their experience, including their level of comfort, satisfaction with the procedure, and any suggestions for improvement. This feedback can help identify areas where adjustments can be made to enhance client safety and comfort. By continuously striving to meet client expectations, piercing studios can establish a reputation for excellence in client care.

Creating a Welcoming Environment
Fostering a welcoming and inclusive environment is essential for client safety and comfort. Piercing studios should strive to create a space where clients feel respected, valued, and comfortable expressing their concerns or preferences. This includes promoting diversity, providing a non-judgmental atmosphere, and respecting clients' privacy and confidentiality.

Compliance with Legal and Ethical Standards
Adhering to legal and ethical standards is crucial for client safety and well-being. Piercing studios should comply with all applicable health and safety regulations, including licensing requirements, age restrictions, and proper record-keeping practices. Respecting clients' rights, privacy, and confidentiality is paramount in maintaining their trust and ensuring their safety.

Collaboration with Healthcare Professionals
Establishing collaborative relationships with healthcare professionals enhances client safety during the piercing process. Piercers should maintain open communication with healthcare providers, such as dermatologists or infectious disease specialists, to seek guidance on specific client cases or potential complications. This collaboration ensures a holistic approach to client care and promotes their overall well-being.

In conclusion, ensuring client safety and comfort is a fundamental aspect of the piercing process. By educating clients, obtaining informed consent, maintaining a hygienic environment, following sterilization practices, employing gentle and precise techniques, and providing comprehensive aftercare instructions, piercing studios can create a safe and comfortable experience for their clients. Ongoing support, continuous professional development, and a commitment to client feedback and satisfaction further contribute to a positive and trusted relationship between the studio and its clients.

8.
Aftercare Instructions for Various Piercings

Proper aftercare is essential for the successful healing and maintenance of piercings. This chapter will provide comprehensive aftercare instructions for various types of piercings, ensuring that clients have the knowledge and guidance they need to promote healing, prevent infections, and maintain the longevity of their piercings.

Ear Piercings
Ear piercings, including lobe, cartilage, and helix piercings, require diligent care to prevent complications. After getting an ear piercing, it's crucial to clean the area twice a day with a saline solution or a mild saline-based cleanser. Gently rotate the jewelry during cleaning to prevent it from sticking to the piercing. Avoid touching the piercing with dirty hands and refrain from changing the jewelry until the piercing has fully healed, which can take several weeks to a few months. It's important to avoid swimming in pools or bodies of water during the healing process to reduce the risk of infection. Be mindful of sleeping positions that may put pressure on the piercing and consider using a travel pillow or a donut-shaped pillow for added comfort.

Facial Piercings

Facial piercings, such as nose, eyebrow, and lip piercings, require special care due to their visibility and the potential for increased exposure to bacteria. Clean the piercing twice a day with a saline solution or a mild, fragrance-free cleanser. Use a cotton swab or clean hands to gently remove any crust or discharge around the piercing. Avoid touching or twisting the jewelry unnecessarily, as this can introduce bacteria and delay healing. When applying skincare products or makeup, be cautious not to get them directly on the piercing. Avoid swimming or submerging the piercing in water, and be careful when drying your face to avoid snagging the jewelry. It's advisable to avoid using alcohol-based products, as they can dry out the skin and delay healing.

Oral Piercings

Oral piercings, such as tongue and lip piercings, require special attention to minimize the risk of infection and promote healing. Rinse the mouth with an alcohol-free mouthwash or a saline solution after eating, drinking, or smoking to keep the piercing clean. Avoid playing with the jewelry, chewing on hard or sticky foods, or engaging in activities that may increase the risk of trauma to the piercing. Practice good oral hygiene by brushing your teeth gently twice a day and using a soft-bristled toothbrush. Avoid alcohol, tobacco, and spicy foods during the initial healing period, as they can irritate the piercing. Regularly check the jewelry for tightness and make sure the balls or ends are securely fastened.

Navel Piercings

Navel piercings require careful care to prevent irritation and promote healing. Clean the piercing twice a day with a saline solution or a mild, fragrance-free cleanser. Gently rotate the jewelry during cleaning to prevent it from adhering to the piercing. Avoid tight clothing that may rub against the piercing and opt for loose, breathable fabrics. Be cautious when engaging in physical activities or exercises that may put strain on the piercing, and consider using a protective cover or padding during contact sports. Avoid swimming or submerging the piercing in water until it is fully healed, which can take several months.

Genital Piercings

Genital piercings, such as nipple, clitoral hood, or Prince Albert piercings, require careful aftercare to prevent infections and promote healing in sensitive areas. Clean the piercing twice a day with a saline solution or a mild, fragrance-free cleanser. Avoid sexual activity during the initial healing period to prevent irritation or trauma to the piercing. If engaging in sexual activity, use barrier methods to reduce the risk of infection. Wear loose-fitting, breathable underwear to minimize friction and promote airflow. Avoid tight clothing that may rub against the piercing and opt for comfortable, non-restrictive clothing. Be mindful of activities that may put strain on the piercing, such as intense physical exercise or sports, and take necessary precautions to protect the piercing during these activities. It's important to communicate openly with sexual partners about the presence of the piercing to ensure their understanding and cooperation in maintaining its cleanliness and safety.

Surface Piercings

Surface piercings, such as nape, collarbone, or wrist piercings, require extra care due to their unique placement. Clean the piercing twice a day with a saline solution or a mild, fragrance-free cleanser. Gently remove any crust or discharge around the piercing using a cotton swab or clean hands. Avoid clothing or accessories that may rub against the piercing and cause irritation. Be cautious when sleeping, as pressure on the piercing can impede healing. Avoid swimming or submerging the piercing in water until it has fully healed, as this can increase the risk of infection. Monitor the piercing closely for signs of migration or rejection, such as increased redness, swelling, or discomfort, and consult with a professional piercer if any concerns arise.

Industrial Piercings

Industrial piercings, which involve two separate holes connected by a long barbell, require careful aftercare to ensure proper healing and alignment. Clean the piercing twice a day with a saline solution or a mild, fragrance-free cleanser. Gently rotate the jewelry during cleaning to prevent it from adhering to the piercing. Avoid sleeping on the side of the piercing to minimize pressure and discomfort. Be cautious when brushing or styling your hair to avoid snagging the jewelry. Avoid changing the jewelry until the piercing has fully healed, which can take several months. It's important to consult with a professional piercer for any necessary adjustments or concerns regarding the alignment or comfort of the jewelry.

Remember, each piercing is unique, and healing times can vary. It's essential to follow these aftercare instructions diligently and consult with a professional piercer if you experience any unusual symptoms, prolonged pain, or signs of infection. By providing proper care and attention to your piercings, you can promote healing, minimize complications, and enjoy your piercings for years to come.

9.
Dealing with Pain and Anxiety in Clients

Introduction:
Dealing with pain and anxiety is a crucial aspect of the piercing process. As piercers, it is essential to understand the concerns and discomfort that clients may experience. By implementing strategies to manage pain and anxiety effectively, we can create a more comfortable and positive experience for our clients. This chapter will explore various techniques and approaches to help clients cope with pain and anxiety during the piercing process.

Understanding Pain Perception:
Pain perception varies among individuals, and it is essential to acknowledge and respect each client's unique pain tolerance. Some clients may have a higher pain threshold, while others may be more sensitive. By engaging in open and honest communication with clients, we can better understand their expectations and concerns regarding pain. This allows us to tailor our approach accordingly and provide appropriate support throughout the process.

Creating a Calm and Supportive Environment:
The environment in which the piercing takes place plays a significant role in managing pain and anxiety. Creating a calm, clean, and welcoming space can help clients feel more at ease. Soft lighting, soothing music, and comfortable seating can contribute to a relaxed atmosphere. Additionally, taking the time to establish a positive rapport with clients, listening to their concerns, and offering reassurance can help alleviate anxiety.

Pre-Piercing Education and Preparation:
Educating clients about the piercing process and what to expect can help alleviate anxiety. Explaining the steps involved, the sensations they may experience, and the duration of the procedure can help set realistic expectations. Providing written materials or resources that clients can review beforehand allows them to familiarize themselves with the process, reducing uncertainty and anxiety. It is also important to answer any questions or address any concerns they may have prior to starting the piercing.

Distraction Techniques:
Distraction techniques can be effective in redirecting clients' attention away from pain or anxiety during the piercing. Engaging in conversation, playing calming music, or having visual distractions, such as artwork or interesting objects, can help divert clients' focus. Some piercers also use handheld devices or gadgets to provide a point of focus for clients during the procedure. By providing a positive distraction, we can help minimize discomfort and anxiety.

Relaxation and Breathing Techniques:
Teaching clients relaxation and breathing techniques can significantly reduce pain and anxiety during the piercing process. Deep breathing exercises, such as inhaling slowly through the nose and exhaling through the mouth, can help promote relaxation and lower stress levels. Encouraging clients to practice these techniques before and during the piercing can help them feel more in control and reduce discomfort.

Topical Anesthetics and Numbing Agents:
In certain cases, the use of topical anesthetics or numbing agents may be appropriate to manage pain during piercings. These products, when used correctly and under professional guidance, can temporarily numb the area, reducing discomfort. However, it is important to assess each client's individual needs and consider any potential risks or allergies before using such products. Proper application and adherence to manufacturer guidelines are crucial to ensure client safety.

Timing and Placement Considerations:
Careful consideration of timing and placement can also contribute to managing pain during piercings. Piercing certain areas during a client's menstrual cycle, when pain sensitivity may be heightened, should be approached with caution. Similarly, selecting appropriate jewelry size and type can minimize discomfort during healing. A thorough assessment of the client's anatomy, preferences, and pain threshold can guide the decision-making process to optimize their comfort.

Post-Piercing Care and Support:
Once the piercing is complete, providing clear aftercare instructions is essential for pain management and healing. Educating clients on proper cleaning techniques, potential discomfort during the healing process, and signs of infection empowers them to take care of their piercings effectively. Being available for follow-up support, addressing any concerns, and providing resources for pain relief, such as saline solutions or recommended over-the-counter pain medications, ensures ongoing comfort and care.

Conclusion:
Dealing with pain and anxiety in clients is a vital aspect of the piercing process. By understanding individual pain perception, creating a supportive environment, and implementing various strategies such as distraction techniques, relaxation exercises, and, when appropriate, topical anesthetics, we can help clients manage discomfort and anxiety effectively. Open communication, education, and ongoing support contribute to a positive piercing experience, fostering trust and satisfaction.

As we continue to explore the topic of dealing with pain and anxiety in clients, let's delve deeper into additional techniques and approaches that can be employed to support clients during the piercing process.

Empathy and Active Listening:
Empathy is a crucial skill in helping clients manage pain and anxiety.
By actively listening to their concerns and acknowledging their
feelings, we can create a safe and understanding environment.
Showing genuine empathy by validating their emotions and expressing
empathy can help build trust and alleviate anxiety. Taking the time to
address their specific worries and providing personalized reassurance
demonstrates our commitment to their well-being.

Visualizations and Guided Imagery:
Visualizations and guided imagery techniques can be effective tools in
pain and anxiety management. By guiding clients through soothing
and positive mental images, we can help redirect their focus and
promote relaxation. Encouraging clients to imagine themselves in a
peaceful and calming setting while engaging in deep breathing
exercises can help reduce discomfort and create a sense of calm
during the piercing process.

Mindfulness and Meditation:
Introducing clients to mindfulness and meditation practices can aid in
pain and anxiety management. Teaching them mindfulness
techniques, such as focusing on the present moment and observing
sensations without judgment, can help shift their attention away from
pain and reduce anxiety. Guided meditation sessions before or during
the piercing process can also be beneficial in promoting relaxation
and increasing their overall sense of well-being.

Collaborative Decision-Making:
Involving clients in the decision-making process regarding their
piercings can help empower them and reduce anxiety. Providing
information about different jewelry options, placement choices, and
potential pain levels associated with each option allows clients to make
informed decisions that align with their preferences and comfort
levels. By including clients in this collaborative process, we can help
alleviate any anxiety related to uncertainty or lack of control.

Supportive Communication:
Maintaining open and supportive communication throughout the entire piercing process is essential. Regularly checking in with clients, providing updates on progress, and addressing any concerns they may have can help alleviate anxiety. Offering words of encouragement and praise during the procedure can also foster a positive atmosphere and boost clients' confidence in their ability to cope with any discomfort.

Alternative Therapies:
In some cases, alternative therapies can complement traditional pain management techniques during the piercing process. Techniques such as acupressure, aromatherapy, or cold therapy can help alleviate pain and reduce anxiety. However, it is important to ensure that these therapies are performed by qualified professionals and do not interfere with the healing process or pose any risks to the client.

Continuing Education and Professional Development:
As piercers, it is essential to stay informed about the latest advancements in pain management techniques and strategies. Continuing education and professional development opportunities, such as attending workshops or conferences, can provide valuable insights and skills to better support clients in managing pain and anxiety. Sharing this knowledge with clients and incorporating evidence-based practices into our procedures can further enhance their experience.

By implementing a combination of these techniques, providing empathetic support, and staying up-to-date with industry advancements, we can create a nurturing and comfortable environment for clients. Remember, every individual's experience with pain and anxiety is unique, and tailoring our approach to meet their specific needs and preferences is key to their satisfaction and well-being.

10.
Local Anesthesia Techniques and their Application

Introduction:
Local anesthesia plays a crucial role in the field of piercing as it provides pain relief and comfort to clients during the procedure. By effectively applying local anesthesia techniques, piercers can minimize discomfort and create a more positive experience for their clients. This chapter will explore various local anesthesia techniques commonly used in piercing and their application.

Understanding Local Anesthesia:
Local anesthesia is a method of pain control that targets a specific area of the body, numbing it to prevent pain sensation. It works by temporarily blocking nerve signals in the area where it is applied, allowing the piercer to perform the procedure with minimal pain or discomfort. Local anesthesia does not affect the client's consciousness, and they remain fully alert during the process.

Topical Anesthesia:
Topical anesthesia is the application of an anesthetic agent directly to the skin or mucous membranes. It is commonly used to numb the surface area before a piercing procedure. The most common topical anesthetic used is a cream or gel containing lidocaine or benzocaine. These anesthetics work by numbing the nerve endings in the applied area, providing temporary relief from pain. It is important to follow the manufacturer's instructions for proper application and duration to ensure client safety.

Infiltration Anesthesia:

Infiltration anesthesia involves injecting a local anesthetic solution directly into the tissue surrounding the piercing site. The solution is typically a combination of a local anesthetic, such as lidocaine or prilocaine, and a vasoconstrictor to reduce bleeding and prolong the anesthetic effect. The piercer carefully injects the solution into the subcutaneous tissue, creating a localized numbing effect. Infiltration anesthesia is commonly used for surface piercings or piercings that involve a small area.

Nerve Block Anesthesia:
Nerve block anesthesia involves targeting a specific nerve or group of nerves that supply sensation to the area being pierced. This technique is typically used for more complex or deep piercings where a larger area needs to be numbed. The piercer locates the nerve(s) using anatomical landmarks or ultrasound guidance and injects the local anesthetic solution near the nerve(s). This blocks the transmission of pain signals from the specific area, providing effective pain relief during the procedure.

Field Block Anesthesia:
Field block anesthesia is similar to nerve block anesthesia but involves injecting the local anesthetic solution around the entire field of the piercing site. This technique provides a wider area of anesthesia, numbing not only the piercing site but also the surrounding tissues. It is commonly used for larger piercings or areas where multiple nerves supply sensation. By numbing a larger area, field block anesthesia ensures comprehensive pain relief and minimizes discomfort for the client.

Combined Techniques:
In some cases, piercers may use a combination of local anesthesia techniques to optimize pain control. For example, a piercer may start with the application of a topical anesthetic to numb the surface area, followed by infiltration or nerve block anesthesia for deeper or larger piercings. By combining techniques, piercers can tailor the anesthesia approach to the specific needs of each client and ensure their comfort throughout the procedure.

Considerations and Safety:
While local anesthesia can greatly enhance the client's experience, it is essential to consider safety precautions and potential risks. Piercers must be trained in the proper administration of local anesthesia techniques to ensure accurate dosing and minimize the risk of complications. Adhering to aseptic techniques, using sterile equipment, and maintaining a sterile field during the procedure is crucial to prevent infection. Additionally, piercers should consider any contraindications or allergies the client may have before administering local anesthesia.

Post-Procedure Care:
After the piercing procedure is complete, it is important to provide proper post-procedure care instructions to the client. They should be informed about potential numbness or discomfort as the anesthesia wears off and advised on how to manage it. Clients should be reminded to avoid chewing on the numbed area, as they may accidentally cause injury due to the lack of sensation. Additionally, they should be educated on signs of infection and instructed to seek professional help if any complications arise.

Conclusion:
Local anesthesia techniques are valuable tools in the field of piercing, providing pain relief and comfort to clients. By understanding and effectively applying topical anesthesia, infiltration anesthesia, nerve block anesthesia, and field block anesthesia, piercers can create a more positive and comfortable experience for their clients. However, it is crucial to prioritize safety, follow proper administration techniques, and provide appropriate post-procedure care to ensure client well-being.

11.
Handling Complications and Risks during the Healing Phase

Complications and risks can sometimes arise during the healing phase of a piercing. It is crucial for both piercers and clients to be aware of these potential issues and know how to handle them effectively. While most piercings heal without significant problems, it is important to be prepared and educated on how to address complications that may occur. This chapter will discuss common complications and risks associated with the healing phase of a piercing, and provide guidance on how to manage them.

Infection is one of the most common complications that can occur during the healing phase of a piercing. Signs of infection include redness, swelling, pain, and the presence of pus. Infections can be caused by bacteria entering the piercing site, often as a result of poor hygiene practices or improper aftercare. To prevent infection, it is crucial to maintain proper hygiene practices, such as cleaning the piercing with a saline solution and avoiding touching the area with dirty hands. If an infection is suspected, clients should be advised to seek medical attention. Treatment may involve antibiotics and proper wound care to promote healing.

Allergic reactions can also occur during the healing phase of a piercing. Some individuals may develop allergies to certain metals used in jewelry, particularly nickel. Allergic reactions can manifest as redness, itching, rash, or even blisters around the piercing site. To prevent allergic reactions, it is important to use high-quality jewelry made from hypoallergenic materials, such as titanium or surgical-grade stainless steel. If an allergic reaction occurs, the jewelry should be removed, and the client should seek medical advice. Switching to alternative materials or avoiding certain allergens can help alleviate the symptoms.

Another complication that can occur is migration or rejection of the piercing. Migration refers to the movement of the jewelry away from its original placement, while rejection refers to the body's rejection of the foreign object (jewelry). These complications can happen due to various factors, including improper placement, poor jewelry quality, or individual body response. If migration or rejection occurs, it is important to assess the situation. In some cases, jewelry repositioning or replacement may be necessary. However, if the piercing is consistently being rejected or causing discomfort, it may be best to remove the jewelry and allow the piercing to close.

Keloids and hypertrophic scars are another concern during the healing phase of a piercing. Keloids are raised, thickened scars that extend beyond the boundaries of the original wound, while hypertrophic scars are raised scars that remain within the wound boundaries. These scars can occur due to an overproduction of collagen during the healing process. It is important to educate clients about the potential for keloid or hypertrophic scar formation, particularly if they have a history of such scarring. Proper wound care, including keeping the piercing clean and avoiding excessive trauma, can help minimize the risk of developing these scars. If keloids or hypertrophic scars do form, medical intervention may be necessary, such as corticosteroid injections or surgical removal.

In some cases, a piercing may develop a bump or granuloma during the healing phase. These bumps can be caused by various factors, such as irritation, infection, or excessive scar tissue formation. It is important to assess the bump and identify the underlying cause. Treatment options may include warm saline compresses, topical medications, or in some cases, removal of the jewelry. It is important to consult with a healthcare professional or an experienced piercer for proper evaluation and guidance.

During the healing phase, it is essential for clients to follow proper aftercare instructions provided by the piercer. This includes cleaning the piercing regularly, avoiding harsh chemicals or products, and avoiding activities that may irritate or damage the piercing. Additionally, clients should be advised to avoid changing or removing the jewelry prematurely, as this can disrupt the healing process and increase the risk of complications.

In conclusion, complications and risks can occur during the healing phase of a piercing. It is important for both piercers and clients to be aware of these potential issues and how to manage them effectively. By promoting proper hygiene practices, using high-quality jewelry, and providing appropriate aftercare instructions, the likelihood of complications can be minimized. However, it is important to address any complications promptly and seek medical advice when necessary to ensure the client's well-being and promote successful healing.

Migration and rejection are additional complications that can occur during the healing phase of a piercing. Migration refers to the movement of the jewelry away from its original placement, while rejection occurs when the body views the jewelry as a foreign object and tries to push it out. These complications can happen due to factors such as improper placement, poor jewelry quality, or individual body response.

If migration or rejection is observed, it is important to assess the situation carefully. In some cases, jewelry repositioning or replacement may be necessary to prevent further complications. It is crucial to monitor the piercing closely and consult with a professional piercer or healthcare provider for guidance. If the piercing is consistently being rejected or causing significant discomfort, it may be best to remove the jewelry and allow the piercing to close naturally.

Keloids and hypertrophic scars are another concern during the healing phase of a piercing. Keloids are raised, thickened scars that extend beyond the boundaries of the original wound, while hypertrophic scars are raised scars that remain within the wound boundaries. These scars can occur due to an overproduction of collagen during the healing process. It is important to educate clients about the potential for keloid or hypertrophic scar formation, particularly if they have a history of such scarring. Proper wound care, including keeping the piercing clean and avoiding excessive trauma, can help minimize the risk of developing these scars. If keloids or hypertrophic scars do form, medical intervention may be necessary, such as corticosteroid injections or surgical removal.

Bumps or granulomas can also develop during the healing phase of a piercing. These bumps can be caused by various factors, such as irritation, infection, or excessive scar tissue formation. It is important to assess the bump and identify the underlying cause. Treatment options may include warm saline compresses, topical medications, or in some cases, removal of the jewelry. It is crucial to consult with a healthcare professional or an experienced piercer for proper evaluation and guidance.

In addition to these complications, clients may also experience discomfort, swelling, or bleeding during the healing phase. These symptoms are typically normal and part of the healing process. However, if the discomfort becomes severe, or if there is excessive swelling or bleeding, it is important to seek professional advice to rule out any complications or infections.

To minimize the risk of complications during the healing phase, it is essential for clients to follow proper aftercare instructions provided by the piercer. This includes cleaning the piercing regularly with a saline solution, avoiding harsh chemicals or products, and avoiding activities that may irritate or damage the piercing. It is also important to avoid changing or removing the jewelry prematurely, as this can disrupt the healing process and increase the risk of complications.

In conclusion, complications and risks can arise during the healing phase of a piercing. By educating clients about potential complications, promoting proper aftercare practices, and addressing any issues promptly, piercers can help minimize the risk and ensure a successful healing process. Regular monitoring, communication with clients, and seeking professional advice when necessary are essential in handling complications and risks effectively.

12.
Selecting Suitable Piercing Jewelry

Choosing the right jewelry for a piercing is crucial for both the client's comfort and the overall success of the piercing. There are various factors to consider when selecting suitable piercing jewelry, including the material, size, style, and appropriate placement. This chapter will provide an in-depth guide on selecting the right jewelry for different types of piercings, ensuring a safe and comfortable experience for the client.

Material Selection:

The choice of material for piercing jewelry is essential to avoid allergic reactions, irritation, or other complications. Some common materials used for piercing jewelry include surgical-grade stainless steel, titanium, niobium, and certain high-quality plastics like PTFE or Bioplast. These materials are known for their biocompatibility and resistance to corrosion. It is important to avoid materials that contain nickel, as nickel allergies are quite common. Clients with known sensitivities to certain metals should consult with their piercer to ensure they choose jewelry made from a suitable material.

Size and Gauge:

Selecting the appropriate size and gauge of jewelry is crucial to ensure a proper fit and promote healing. Jewelry that is too small or too large can cause discomfort, migration, or even rejection of the piercing. The size and gauge of the jewelry should be determined by the piercer based on factors such as the individual's anatomy, the type of piercing, and the desired aesthetic. It is important to follow the piercer's recommendations and avoid changing the jewelry prematurely, as it can disrupt the healing process.

Style and Design:

Piercing jewelry comes in various styles and designs to suit individual preferences and fashion choices. From simple studs to elaborate hoops and dangles, there is a wide range of options available. When selecting the style and design of jewelry, it is important to consider the type of piercing and the desired look. For example, a small stud or hoop may be more suitable for a nostril piercing, while a barbell or captive bead ring may be ideal for a navel piercing. It is crucial to choose jewelry that not only looks aesthetically pleasing but also provides comfort and functionality.

Appropriate Placement:

The placement of the jewelry is essential for both the visual appeal and the overall comfort of the piercing. Different types of piercings have specific recommended placements to ensure optimal healing and minimize the risk of complications. It is important to consult with an experienced piercer who can accurately determine the appropriate placement based on the client's anatomy and the type of piercing. Proper placement ensures that the jewelry sits comfortably and enhances the overall appearance of the piercing.

Jewelry Care and Maintenance:

Once the suitable piercing jewelry has been selected and inserted, proper care and maintenance are crucial for the health and longevity of the piercing. It is important to follow the aftercare instructions provided by the piercer, which may include cleaning the piercing with a saline solution, avoiding excessive touching or rotating of the jewelry, and refraining from exposing the piercing to harsh chemicals or excessive moisture. Regular cleaning and inspection of the jewelry are necessary to prevent the buildup of bacteria or debris that can lead to infection or irritation.

Conclusion:

Selecting suitable piercing jewelry is a vital step in the piercing process. By considering factors such as material, size, style, and appropriate placement, clients can ensure a comfortable and visually pleasing piercing experience. Working with an experienced piercer and following proper aftercare instructions are essential to maintain the health and longevity of the piercing. Remember, the right jewelry not only enhances the beauty of the piercing but also contributes to its overall success.

13.
Materials, Sizes, Shapes, and Styles of Piercing Jewelry

Choosing the right jewelry for a piercing is essential for ensuring the comfort of the client and the overall success of the piercing. There are several factors to consider when selecting suitable piercing jewelry, including the material, size, style, and appropriate placement. This chapter will provide a comprehensive guide to selecting the right jewelry for different types of piercings, ensuring a safe and enjoyable experience for the client.

Material Selection:

The choice of material is crucial when it comes to piercing jewelry to avoid allergic reactions, irritations, or other complications. Common materials used for piercing jewelry include surgical-grade stainless steel, titanium, niobium, and certain high-quality plastics like PTFE or Bioplast. These materials are known for their biocompatibility and resistance to corrosion. It is important to avoid materials that contain nickel, as nickel allergies are quite common. Clients with known sensitivities to certain metals should consult with their piercer to ensure they choose jewelry made from a suitable material.

Size and Gauge:

Selecting the appropriate size and gauge of jewelry is crucial to ensure a proper fit and promote healing. Jewelry that is too small or too large can cause discomfort, migration, or even rejection of the piercing. The size and gauge of the jewelry should be determined by the piercer based on factors such as the individual's anatomy, the type of piercing, and the desired aesthetic. It is important to follow the piercer's recommendations and avoid changing the jewelry prematurely, as it can disrupt the healing process.

Style and Design:

Piercing jewelry comes in various styles and designs to suit individual preferences and fashion choices. From simple studs to elaborate hoops and dangles, there is a wide range of options available. When selecting the style and design of jewelry, it is important to consider the type of piercing and the desired look. For example, a small stud or hoop may be more suitable for a nostril piercing, while a barbell or captive bead ring may be ideal for a navel piercing. It is crucial to choose jewelry that not only looks aesthetically pleasing but also provides comfort and functionality.

Appropriate Placement:

The placement of the jewelry is essential for both the visual appeal and the overall comfort of the piercing. Different types of piercings have specific recommended placements to ensure optimal healing and minimize the risk of complications. It is important to consult with an experienced piercer who can accurately determine the appropriate placement based on the client's anatomy and the type of piercing. Proper placement ensures that the jewelry sits comfortably and enhances the overall appearance of the piercing.

Jewelry Care and Maintenance:

Once the suitable piercing jewelry has been selected and inserted, proper care and maintenance are crucial for the health and longevity of the piercing. It is important to follow the aftercare instructions provided by the piercer, which may include cleaning the piercing with a saline solution, avoiding excessive touching or rotating of the jewelry, and refraining from exposing the piercing to harsh chemicals or excessive moisture. Regular cleaning and inspection of the jewelry are necessary to prevent the buildup of bacteria or debris that can lead to infection or irritation.

Conclusion:

Selecting suitable piercing jewelry is a vital step in the piercing process. By considering factors such as material, size, style, and appropriate placement, clients can ensure a comfortable and visually pleasing piercing experience. Working with an experienced piercer and following proper aftercare instructions are essential to maintain the health and longevity of the piercing. Remember, the right jewelry not only enhances the beauty of the piercing but also contributes to its overall success.

Choosing the Right Jewelry for Specific Piercings:

Different types of piercings require specific types of jewelry to ensure a proper fit and minimize the risk of complications. Let's explore some popular types of piercings and the suitable jewelry options for each:

Ear Piercings:

Earlobe Piercing: Earlobe piercings are the most common and can accommodate a wide variety of jewelry styles, such as studs, hoops, and dangles. It's important to choose jewelry with a comfortable backing that doesn't dig into the skin.
Cartilage Piercing: Cartilage piercings, including helix, tragus, and conch piercings, often require jewelry with a smaller gauge and a flat back or a curved barbell to fit the curved shape of the ear.
Facial Piercings:

Nose Piercing: Nose piercings can be adorned with studs or hoops. It's important to choose jewelry that fits snugly without putting too much pressure on the delicate nasal tissue.
Eyebrow Piercing: Eyebrow piercings typically use curved barbells or captive bead rings. The jewelry should be long enough to accommodate any swelling that may occur during the healing process.

Lip Piercing: Lip piercings, such as labret or Monroe piercings, often use labret studs or captive bead rings. It's crucial to choose jewelry with the appropriate length and size to prevent discomfort or injury to the gums and teeth.
Body Piercings:

Navel Piercing: Navel piercings usually require curved barbells or circular barbells that fit comfortably around the navel area.
Nipple Piercing: Nipple piercings can be adorned with barbells or captive bead rings. It's essential to choose jewelry that is the right size and gauge to prevent migration or irritation.
Genital Piercings:

Male Genital Piercings: Male genital piercings, such as Prince Albert or frenulum piercings, often use curved barbells or captive bead rings. It's important to choose jewelry that provides ample room for movement and comfort.
Female Genital Piercings: Female genital piercings, such as clitoral hood or inner labia piercings, can be adorned with captive bead rings or curved barbells. Comfort and ease of cleaning are key considerations when selecting jewelry for these piercings.
Remember, the choice of jewelry for any piercing should be made in consultation with an experienced piercer. They will consider your anatomy, lifestyle, and healing process to recommend the most suitable jewelry options.

14.
Safely Changing Piercing Jewelry

Changing your piercing jewelry can be an exciting way to refresh your look and express your style. However, it's important to approach the process with caution to avoid complications and ensure a safe and successful jewelry change. Here are some detailed guidelines to follow when changing your piercing jewelry:

Prepare Properly:
Before you begin the jewelry change, it's crucial to prepare yourself and create a clean and hygienic environment. Follow these steps to prepare properly:

Start by washing your hands thoroughly with soap and warm water. This will help eliminate any potential bacteria or dirt that could be transferred to your piercing.
Clean the area around the piercing using a saline solution or a mild, fragrance-free cleanser. Gently remove any debris or buildup to ensure a clean surface for the jewelry change.
Gather all the necessary tools and supplies you'll need for the process, such as sterile gloves, cotton swabs, and the new jewelry piece. Having everything ready will help streamline the process and minimize the risk of contamination.
Choose the Right Time:
Timing is important when it comes to changing your piercing jewelry. Consider the following factors before proceeding:

Make sure your piercing is fully healed before attempting to change the jewelry. Healing times can vary depending on the type of piercing, so it's best to consult with your piercer for guidance.
Avoid changing jewelry during periods of heightened activity or stress. It's important to have a calm and focused mindset during the process to minimize the risk of accidents or mishaps.

If you have any concerns or doubts about changing the jewelry yourself, it's always a good idea to seek professional assistance from your piercer. They have the expertise to guide you through the process and ensure a safe jewelry change.

Be Gentle and Patient:

Changing your piercing jewelry requires a gentle and patient approach to avoid discomfort or damage. Follow these steps to ensure a smooth process:

Use sterile gloves or clean hands to handle the new jewelry. This helps maintain a clean and hygienic environment for the jewelry change.

Carefully remove the existing jewelry by unscrewing or sliding it out, depending on the type of jewelry. Avoid any forceful movements or pulling, as this can cause unnecessary pain or damage to the piercing.

Cleanse both the jewelry and the area around the piercing using a saline solution or a mild cleanser. This helps remove any residue or bacteria that may have accumulated.

When inserting the new jewelry, take your time and be patient. Follow the natural direction of the piercing hole and gently guide the jewelry in. Avoid any forceful or abrupt movements that could cause discomfort or injury.

Choose Appropriate Jewelry:

Selecting the right jewelry for your piercing is crucial for both comfort and safety. Consider the following factors when choosing your new jewelry:

Opt for jewelry made from safe and suitable materials for your piercing. Surgical steel and titanium are commonly recommended for their hypoallergenic properties and compatibility with most piercings. If you have known metal allergies or sensitivities, avoid jewelry containing nickel or other problematic metals.

Ensure the new jewelry has the correct gauge, length, and style for your specific piercing. Consult with your piercer if you're unsure about the sizing or style options. They can provide valuable guidance based on their expertise and knowledge.

Take into account your personal preferences and style. Whether you prefer simple and understated designs or bold and intricate pieces, choose jewelry that reflects your individuality and enhances your overall look.

Monitor for Signs of Irritation or Infection:

After changing your piercing jewelry, it's important to monitor your piercing for any signs of irritation or infection. Here's what you should keep in mind:

Pay attention to any redness, swelling, excessive pain, or unusual discharge from the piercing site. These could be signs of an infection or an adverse reaction to the new jewelry.

If you experience discomfort or notice any abnormal symptoms, it's advisable to consult with your piercer or a healthcare professional for further evaluation and guidance.

Continue practicing proper aftercare routines for your piercing, such as cleaning the area with a saline solution and avoiding harsh chemicals or irritants. Maintaining good hygiene and caring for your piercing will help promote proper healing and minimize the risk of complications.

By following these detailed guidelines and taking the necessary precautions, you can safely change your piercing jewelry, enjoy a fresh look, and maintain the health and integrity of your piercing.

15.
Customer Communication and Consultation Skills

Developing strong customer communication and consultation skills is essential for professionals in the piercing industry. Building trust, understanding clients' needs, and effectively conveying information are key to providing exceptional service and ensuring customer satisfaction. Here are some detailed aspects to consider when it comes to customer communication and consultation:

Active Listening:
Active listening is a fundamental skill for effective communication. It involves fully engaging with the customer, paying close attention to their verbal and non-verbal cues, and showing genuine interest in their concerns and desires. Active listening techniques include maintaining eye contact, nodding to show understanding, and asking probing questions to gather more information. By actively listening, you can establish a connection with the customer, demonstrate empathy, and address their specific needs.

Empathy and Understanding:
Empathy is the ability to understand and share the feelings of another person. It is crucial in the piercing industry, as customers may have fears, concerns, or specific expectations. Showing empathy helps create a supportive and comfortable environment for clients. Acknowledge their emotions, validate their experiences, and assure them that their feelings are heard and respected. By demonstrating empathy, you can build trust and enhance the customer's overall experience.

Clear and Effective Communication:
Clear and effective communication is vital to ensure that clients understand the information and instructions provided to them. Use language that is easily understood by the customer, avoiding technical jargon or complex terms. Speak clearly and at an appropriate pace, allowing customers to process the information. When explaining procedures, aftercare instructions, or jewelry options, use visual aids, diagrams, or demonstrations to enhance comprehension. Be open to answering any questions the customer may have and provide additional clarification as needed.

Educating and Informing:
As a professional piercer, it is important to educate and inform clients about the various aspects of piercings. This includes discussing different piercing types, potential risks, aftercare routines, and suitable jewelry options. Provide detailed explanations about the piercing process, including preparation, the importance of proper hygiene, and potential complications. Discuss the expected healing time and any potential discomfort that the customer may experience. Empower customers by sharing knowledge, allowing them to make informed decisions and actively participate in their piercing journey.

Managing Expectations:
Managing customer expectations is a crucial part of the consultation process. Be honest and transparent about the limitations of certain piercings, potential risks, and realistic outcomes. Discuss any potential discomfort, healing times, and the importance of following aftercare instructions. By managing expectations, you can prevent misunderstandings and ensure that customers have a realistic understanding of the process.

Conflict Resolution:
In some cases, conflicts or misunderstandings may arise during the consultation or after the piercing. It is important to handle these situations with professionalism and empathy. Actively listen to the customer's concerns, allowing them to express their grievances fully. Show understanding and validate their feelings. Work together to find a solution that satisfies the customer and aligns with industry standards and safety protocols. Effective conflict resolution can turn a negative experience into a positive one and strengthen the customer's trust in your professionalism.

By honing your customer communication and consultation skills, you can create a welcoming and informative environment for your clients. Effective communication, active listening, empathy, clear explanations, and managing expectations are key factors in ensuring customer satisfaction and building long-term relationships.

16.
Managing Different Customer Types and Needs

In the piercing industry, professionals encounter a diverse range of customers with unique preferences, needs, and personalities. Effectively managing different customer types is crucial for providing exceptional service and ensuring customer satisfaction. Let's explore some common customer types and strategies for meeting their specific needs:

The Indecisive Customer:
This customer type may struggle with making decisions, particularly when it comes to choosing the right piercing or jewelry. They appreciate guidance and reassurance. Take the time to understand their preferences and concerns. Provide a variety of options, explain the features and benefits of each, and offer your professional opinion when needed. Help them visualize how different choices would look and ensure they feel confident in their decision.

The Nervous Customer:
These customers often experience anxiety or nervousness before getting a piercing. It's important to create a calm and supportive environment for them. Take the time to explain the process step by step, addressing any concerns they may have. Offer reassurance and share stories of successful piercings to help alleviate their fears. Use gentle and comforting language throughout the procedure to help them relax.

The Detail-Oriented Customer:
This customer type pays attention to the smallest details and may ask specific questions about the procedure, aftercare, and jewelry options. They appreciate thorough explanations and factual information. Take the time to provide detailed answers to their questions, using visual aids if necessary. Help them understand the different aspects of the piercing process, including healing times, aftercare routines, and potential risks. Provide them with reliable sources of information to further their knowledge.

The Trendsetter:
These customers are always seeking the latest trends and unique styles. They appreciate being presented with a wide range of fashionable and cutting-edge jewelry designs. Stay up-to-date with current piercing trends and offer a diverse selection of stylish options. Provide recommendations based on their personal style and preferences. Encourage their creativity and offer customized options to help them achieve a unique and on-trend look.

The First-Time Customer:
First-time customers may be unfamiliar with the piercing process and have specific concerns about pain, healing, and aftercare. They appreciate clear and comprehensive information. Take the time to educate them about the entire process, from preparation to aftercare. Address their concerns and explain the common sensations they may experience during and after the piercing. Provide detailed aftercare instructions and emphasize the importance of following them for proper healing.

The Well-Informed Customer:
These customers have already done their research and have a good understanding of piercings, aftercare practices, and jewelry options. They appreciate knowledgeable professionals who can engage in meaningful discussions about their preferences and desired outcome. Acknowledge their knowledge and offer additional insights or recommendations to enhance their understanding. Provide personalized recommendations based on their specific requirements and preferences.

The Adventurous Customer:
This customer type is open to exploring unique and unconventional piercings. They seek guidance on more daring choices and appreciate professionals who can provide expert advice. Engage in conversations about their desired piercing, discussing the feasibility, potential risks, and aftercare requirements. Offer a wide range of jewelry options that are suitable for their chosen piercing, while ensuring they understand the importance of proper aftercare and follow-up appointments.

By understanding and adapting to the needs of different customer types, you can create a personalized and satisfactory experience for each individual. Patience, empathy, clear communication, and expertise are key in effectively managing different customer types. Remember, each customer is unique, and providing tailored attention and guidance will help build trust and loyalty.

17.
Customer Retention and Building a Loyal Client Base

In the piercing industry, building a loyal client base is crucial for long-term success. Satisfied customers not only become repeat clients but also act as advocates, spreading positive word-of-mouth and attracting new business. Here are some strategies to enhance customer retention and cultivate a loyal client base:

Consistent and Personalized Service:
Consistency is key when it comes to providing excellent customer service. It's important to consistently deliver a high level of service throughout the entire customer journey. From the moment a client walks into your studio or contacts you for inquiries, ensure that they receive a warm and welcoming experience. Address clients by name and engage in personalized conversations to build rapport. Remembering their preferences, such as their preferred jewelry style or aftercare routine, shows that you value their individual needs and preferences.

Communication and Follow-up:
Maintaining open and clear communication with clients is essential. Promptly respond to inquiries and provide detailed and accurate information. Be attentive and actively listen to their concerns, questions, and feedback. After a piercing, follow up with clients to check on their satisfaction and address any post-piercing issues or concerns they may have. This level of follow-up demonstrates your commitment to their well-being and helps to build trust and loyalty.

VIP Programs and Loyalty Rewards:
Implementing a VIP program or loyalty rewards system can encourage repeat business and foster loyalty among your clients. Offer exclusive benefits to clients who join the program, such as discounts on future piercings or jewelry purchases, priority booking for appointments, or access to limited-edition pieces. Consider tiered rewards based on client engagement or spending levels to provide incentives for clients to reach higher tiers and enjoy even greater benefits.

Ongoing Education and Information:
Providing ongoing education and information to your clients helps to establish you as a trusted expert in the field. Share educational materials, such as brochures or online resources, that cover topics such as aftercare instructions, jewelry options, and common piercing concerns. Use social media platforms, newsletters, or blog posts to regularly share informative content, including tips, trends, and FAQs. By keeping your clients informed and empowered with knowledge, you demonstrate your commitment to their well-being and foster a sense of trust and loyalty.

Special Events and Exclusive Offers:
Hosting special events and offering exclusive promotions or discounts can create excitement and engagement among your loyal clients. Consider organizing client appreciation nights where clients can enjoy special perks such as complimentary consultations, discounts on jewelry purchases, or even small gifts. Offer limited-edition jewelry collections or collaborate with local artists to create unique pieces exclusively available to your clients. These events and offers create a sense of exclusivity and strengthen the bond between you and your loyal clients.

Referral Programs:
Harness the power of word-of-mouth marketing by implementing a referral program. Encourage your satisfied clients to refer their friends, family, and acquaintances to your services. Incentivize referrals by offering rewards or incentives to both the referring client and the new client they bring in. This can be in the form of discounts on future services or jewelry, free add-on services, or special gifts. Provide referral cards or unique referral codes that clients can easily share with their network, making it convenient for them to spread the word about your business and bring in new clients.

Continuous Improvement and Innovation:
Staying current with industry trends and continuously improving your services is vital for building customer loyalty. Stay updated on the latest techniques, jewelry options, and aftercare practices. Attend conferences, workshops, or seminars to expand your knowledge and skills. Actively seek client feedback through surveys or face-to-face conversations to identify areas for improvement. Regularly evaluate your offerings and make enhancements based on client feedback and market demands. By consistently striving for improvement and embracing innovation, you demonstrate your commitment to delivering exceptional experiences to your clients.

Building a loyal client base takes time, effort, and dedication. By providing consistent and personalized service, maintaining open communication, implementing loyalty programs, referral incentives, and continuously improving your offerings, you can foster strong relationships with your clients and ensure their long-term loyalty. Remember, happy clients not only become repeat customers but also your best ambassadors, helping you attract new business and establish yourself as a trusted professional in the industry.

18.
Legal Regulations and Best Practices for Piercing

The field of piercing is subject to various legal regulations and best practices to ensure the safety and well-being of both the piercer and the client. Adhering to these regulations and best practices is crucial for maintaining professionalism, promoting a positive reputation, and providing high-quality services. In this chapter, we will delve into the detailed legal considerations and best practices that piercers should follow to ensure compliance and create a safe environment for their clients.

Legal Regulations:

Licensing and Certification:
Piercers must comply with specific licensing and certification requirements set by local, state, and national authorities. These requirements often involve completing training programs, obtaining permits, and passing examinations to demonstrate proficiency in safe piercing techniques. It is essential for piercers to thoroughly research and understand the legal requirements in their jurisdiction to ensure compliance.

Age Restrictions:
Piercing minors requires additional attention and adherence to specific regulations. In many jurisdictions, parental consent is necessary for individuals under a certain age to get pierced. Moreover, certain types of piercings, such as genital or nipple piercings, may have specific age restrictions in place. Piercers must verify identification, obtain consent forms from parents or guardians, and follow the legal requirements regarding age restrictions to protect both the minor and the piercer.

Health and Safety Standards:
Maintaining a clean and safe environment is of utmost importance in the piercing industry. Piercers must adhere to rigorous health and safety standards to ensure the well-being of their clients. This includes proper sterilization of tools and equipment, use of single-use disposable needles and jewelry, and implementation of infection control measures. It is vital for piercers to stay updated on industry standards and guidelines provided by professional piercing organizations or health regulatory agencies.

Record-Keeping:
Accurate and thorough record-keeping is essential for legal and health purposes. Piercers should maintain detailed records of each client, including their personal information, the type of piercing, the jewelry used, and any relevant medical history or allergies. These records not only demonstrate compliance with legal regulations but also serve as a reference for future follow-ups or inquiries. Proper record-keeping is crucial for maintaining transparency, accountability, and professionalism.

Best Practices:

Informed Consent:
Obtaining informed consent from clients is not only an ethical obligation but also a legal requirement. Piercers should provide comprehensive information about the piercing procedure, potential risks and complications, aftercare instructions, and the expected healing process. It is essential for clients to have a clear understanding of the procedure and actively consent to it before the piercing takes place. Piercers may utilize written consent forms to document this process.

Client Education:
Educating clients about proper aftercare practices is essential for their well-being and the success of the piercing. Piercers should provide detailed instructions on cleaning, hygiene, and potential complications. By educating clients, piercers empower them to take responsibility for their own health and ensure that they are equipped with the knowledge and understanding necessary to care for their piercing properly. Ongoing education and support contribute to successful healing and client satisfaction.

Continuous Professional Development:
Piercers should prioritize continuous professional development to stay up-to-date with the latest techniques, industry trends, and best practices. This can include attending workshops, conferences, or seminars, as well as staying informed through professional publications and online resources. Continuous learning not only enhances the skills and knowledge of piercers but also enables them to provide the best possible service to their clients. It ensures compliance with changing regulations, promotes innovation, and fosters professional growth.

Effective Communication and Documentation:
Clear and effective communication with clients is crucial throughout the entire piercing process. This includes discussing their expectations, addressing any concerns or questions they may have, and providing detailed aftercare instructions. Additionally, maintaining comprehensive documentation of client interactions, consent forms, and aftercare instructions is vital. These records not only protect both the piercer and the client but also serve as evidence of professionalism, adherence to best practices, and compliance with legal regulations.

Implementing legal regulations and following best practices is essential for piercers to provide a safe and professional environment for their clients. By obtaining the necessary licenses and certifications, following age restrictions, maintaining health and safety standards, practicing informed consent, continuously developing their skills, and maintaining effective communication and documentation, piercers can uphold their ethical and legal responsibilities. These actions contribute to a positive and satisfactory piercing experience for clients while fostering trust, loyalty, and a strong reputation within the industry.

19.
Licensing and Certification for Piercers

Piercing is a specialized skill that requires knowledge, training, and expertise to perform safely and effectively. To ensure the highest standards of professionalism and safety within the industry, licensing and certification play a crucial role. In this chapter, we will explore the importance of licensing and certification for piercers, the requirements and processes involved, and the benefits they provide to both piercers and their clients.

The Importance of Licensing and Certification

Licensing and certification serve as a recognition of a piercer's competence and adherence to industry standards. They provide assurance to clients that the piercer has met certain qualifications and possesses the necessary skills and knowledge to perform piercings safely. By obtaining the appropriate licenses and certifications, piercers demonstrate their commitment to professionalism, continuous learning, and client safety.

Requirements for Licensing and Certification

The requirements for licensing and certification vary depending on the jurisdiction and the specific organizations or governing bodies overseeing the process. However, common requirements often include:

Training Programs: Piercers are typically required to complete training programs that cover essential topics such as hygiene, sterilization techniques, anatomy, piercing procedures, aftercare, and health and safety regulations. These programs may be offered by accredited institutions, professional piercing organizations, or certified trainers.

Practical Experience: Alongside formal training, many licensing and certification processes require piercers to gain a certain amount of practical experience under the guidance of experienced mentors or trainers. This hands-on experience allows piercers to apply their knowledge in real-world scenarios and develop the necessary skills for safe and effective piercing.

Written Examinations: Piercers may need to pass written examinations that assess their understanding of piercing techniques, hygiene practices, anatomy, jewelry selection, aftercare protocols, and relevant health regulations. These examinations test the piercer's knowledge and ensure they are equipped with the necessary information to provide high-quality services.

Bloodborne Pathogen Training: Given the potential risks associated with bloodborne pathogens, many jurisdictions require piercers to undergo specialized training on infection control, bloodborne pathogens, and safe handling and disposal of contaminated materials. This training ensures that piercers have the knowledge and skills to minimize the risk of infections and cross-contamination.

Benefits of Licensing and Certification

Licensing and certification offer several benefits to both piercers and their clients:

Professionalism: Holding a valid license or certification demonstrates a piercer's commitment to professionalism and adherence to industry standards. It enhances their reputation and instills confidence in clients, making them more likely to choose a licensed and certified piercer for their piercing needs.

Client Safety: Licensing and certification ensure that piercers are knowledgeable about proper hygiene practices, sterilization techniques, and health regulations. This knowledge and training significantly reduce the risk of infections, complications, and other potential risks associated with piercing. Clients can feel confident that their safety is a top priority when working with a licensed and certified piercer.

Legal Compliance: Licensing and certification help piercers comply with local, state, and national regulations governing the practice of piercing. By obtaining the necessary licenses and certifications, piercers avoid legal issues and potential penalties. They also contribute to the overall integrity and reputation of the piercing industry.

Continuous Learning: Many licensing and certification programs require piercers to engage in ongoing education and professional development. This ensures that piercers stay updated on the latest techniques, industry trends, and health and safety practices. Continuous learning enables piercers to provide the best possible service to their clients and adapt to evolving industry standards.

In conclusion, licensing and certification are essential for piercers to demonstrate their professionalism, competence, and commitment to client safety. By fulfilling the requirements set by the appropriate licensing bodies, piercers enhance their reputation, comply with legal regulations, and provide clients with a safe and high-quality piercing experience. Licensing and certification contribute to the overall growth and advancement of the piercing industry, ensuring that piercers meet the highest standards of excellence.

20.
Piercing on Minors and Parental Consent in Law

Piercing on minors is a topic that requires careful consideration and adherence to legal regulations to ensure the well-being and safety of young individuals. In many jurisdictions, there are specific laws and guidelines in place regarding the piercing of minors, including the requirement of parental consent. This chapter will explore the legal framework surrounding piercing on minors and the importance of obtaining parental consent.

Legal Age Restrictions:
One of the fundamental aspects of piercing on minors is the establishment of legal age restrictions. The age at which a minor can legally consent to a piercing varies from jurisdiction to jurisdiction. In some places, the age may be as low as 16, while in others, it may be 18 or even higher. It is essential for piercers to familiarize themselves with the specific age restrictions in their jurisdiction to ensure compliance with the law.

Parental Consent:
Parental consent is a critical aspect of piercing on minors. In most jurisdictions, parents or legal guardians must provide written consent for a minor to undergo a piercing procedure. This consent serves as evidence that the parents are aware of and have approved the piercing, taking into account potential risks, aftercare requirements, and any potential complications that may arise. Piercers must have a thorough understanding of the legal requirements regarding parental consent and maintain proper documentation of consent forms.

Informed Decision-Making:
In addition to obtaining parental consent, it is essential to ensure that both the minor and the parents have a clear understanding of the piercing procedure, including its risks, benefits, and aftercare requirements. Piercers should take the time to explain the process thoroughly, answer any questions or concerns, and provide educational materials or resources to aid in the decision-making process. This informed decision-making allows the minor and their parents to make an educated choice regarding the piercing and fosters trust and transparency in the piercer-client relationship.

Safety Considerations:
When performing a piercing on a minor, piercers must prioritize safety and take additional precautions to ensure a safe and hygienic environment. This includes adhering to strict sterilization protocols, using single-use disposable needles and sterile equipment, and following proper infection control measures. The piercer must have the necessary knowledge and skills to handle the unique needs and potential challenges associated with piercing on minors, such as their smaller anatomy and potential discomfort during the procedure.

Educating Parents and Minors:
Piercers play a vital role in educating both parents and minors about the piercing process, aftercare instructions, and potential risks. This education should include information on proper cleaning and hygiene practices, signs of infection or complications to watch out for, and the importance of seeking professional help if any issues arise. By providing comprehensive education, piercers empower parents and minors to make informed decisions and ensure proper care and healing after the piercing.

Legal Consequences and Professional Liability:
Failure to comply with legal age restrictions and obtain proper
parental consent can have serious consequences for piercers. Legal
repercussions may include fines, suspension or revocation of licenses,
or even criminal charges, depending on the jurisdiction. Additionally,
piercers may face professional liability if they perform a piercing on a
minor without consent or in violation of legal requirements. It is
crucial for piercers to familiarize themselves with the legal
consequences and take the necessary steps to ensure compliance.

In conclusion, piercing on minors requires adherence to legal
regulations, including obtaining parental consent and complying with
age restrictions. Piercers must understand and follow the specific laws
and guidelines in their jurisdiction to ensure the safety and well-being
of both minors and their parents. By providing thorough education,
maintaining proper documentation, and prioritizing safety, piercers
can uphold their ethical and legal responsibilities and contribute to a
positive and safe piercing experience for minors.

21.
Piercing during Pregnancy and Breastfeeding

Piercing during pregnancy and breastfeeding is a topic that requires careful consideration and understanding of the potential risks and considerations for both the individual and the developing baby. While the decision to get pierced during these periods is ultimately a personal one, it is important to be well-informed and make choices that prioritize the health and well-being of both the parent and the child. In this chapter, we will explore the various factors to consider when contemplating piercing during pregnancy and breastfeeding.

Piercing during Pregnancy:
During pregnancy, the body undergoes numerous physiological changes, and these changes can impact the healing process and overall well-being. It is generally recommended to avoid getting pierced during pregnancy, especially in the later stages, due to the increased risk of complications and discomfort.

One important consideration is the healing and recovery process. Piercings require proper healing time, and the body's ability to heal may be compromised during pregnancy due to hormonal changes and increased blood flow. It is essential to prioritize the health and safety of both the individual and the developing baby, which may mean postponing any new piercings until after the pregnancy.

Another consideration is the increased risk of infection and complications. Pregnancy can weaken the immune system, making individuals more susceptible to infections. Piercings create an open wound that can increase the risk of infection. It is crucial to maintain excellent hygiene and consult with a healthcare professional before considering any piercing during pregnancy.

Additionally, the comfort level should be taken into account. As the body undergoes changes, piercings may become more uncomfortable or even painful. Swelling, tenderness, and changes in the breast or abdominal area can affect the comfort level of existing piercings. It is essential to listen to your body and prioritize your comfort during this time.

Piercing during Breastfeeding:
Breastfeeding is a special time that requires extra caution when it comes to piercing. Considerations for piercing during breastfeeding include the choice of jewelry material, the location and accessibility of the piercing, and proper hygiene and cleaning routines.

Choosing piercing jewelry made from safe and non-reactive materials is crucial to minimize any potential harm to the baby. Materials such as surgical steel, titanium, or biocompatible plastics are generally considered safe choices. It is important to consult with a professional piercer who is knowledgeable about safe materials for breastfeeding individuals.

The placement of the piercing is also important during breastfeeding. Piercings on or near the breasts or nipples can interfere with proper latching and breastfeeding. It is essential to consult with a lactation specialist or healthcare professional to ensure that the piercing does not pose any challenges to breastfeeding. They can provide guidance on the appropriate placement and offer solutions if there are any issues.

Maintaining proper hygiene and cleaning routines is essential to prevent infection and ensure the well-being of both the parent and the baby. Regular cleaning of the piercing site, along with proper hand hygiene, is necessary to minimize the risk of any complications. It is important to follow the recommended cleaning instructions provided by the piercer or healthcare professional.

Consulting with Healthcare Professionals:
Throughout pregnancy and breastfeeding, it is essential to maintain open communication with healthcare professionals, such as obstetricians, midwives, and lactation consultants. These professionals can provide personalized advice based on individual circumstances and help make informed decisions regarding piercing during these periods. They can offer guidance on the potential risks and considerations specific to each individual and provide support throughout the journey.

In conclusion, the decision to get pierced during pregnancy and breastfeeding is a personal one that should prioritize the health and well-being of both the parent and the child. It is crucial to consider the potential risks, consult with healthcare professionals, and make informed decisions based on individual circumstances. Ultimately, the safety and comfort of both the parent and the baby should be the top priority.

22.
Special Precautions and Risks for Specific Groups

When it comes to piercing, certain groups of people may require special considerations and precautions due to their unique characteristics or health conditions. It is essential for piercers to be aware of these factors and adapt their practices accordingly to ensure the safety and well-being of their clients. In this chapter, we will explore some specific groups that may require special precautions and the associated risks.

Pregnant Individuals:
Pregnant individuals should approach piercing with caution due to the potential impact on both their own health and the health of the developing fetus. Hormonal changes, increased blood flow, and changes in the body's immune response during pregnancy can affect the healing process and increase the risk of complications. Piercers should carefully evaluate the risks and consult with the individual's healthcare provider before proceeding with any piercings.

Children and Minors:
Piercing children and minors requires extra care and attention. In many jurisdictions, parental consent is required for individuals under a certain age to get pierced. Piercers should obtain written consent from parents or legal guardians and ensure that the piercing is appropriate for the child's age and maturity level. It is crucial to create a comfortable and safe environment for young clients and to provide age-appropriate aftercare instructions to both the child and their parents.

Elderly Individuals:
Elderly individuals may have unique considerations when it comes to piercing due to factors such as thinning skin, reduced collagen production, and slower healing processes. Piercers should take extra care to minimize trauma to the skin and choose appropriate jewelry sizes and materials to accommodate the specific needs of older clients. Clear communication and realistic expectations regarding healing times and potential risks are also important for this age group.

Individuals with Medical Conditions:
People with underlying medical conditions may need to take special precautions before getting pierced. Certain health conditions, such as diabetes, autoimmune disorders, and bleeding disorders, can affect the body's ability to heal and increase the risk of complications. Piercers should consult with the individual's healthcare provider to assess the risks, ensure proper wound care, and determine if any modifications or restrictions are necessary.

Immunocompromised Individuals:
Individuals with compromised immune systems, such as those with HIV/AIDS, undergoing chemotherapy, or taking immunosuppressive medications, have an increased risk of infection and delayed healing. Piercers should take extra precautions to maintain strict hygiene practices, use sterile equipment, and provide comprehensive aftercare instructions to minimize the risk of infection and promote optimal healing. Consulting with the individual's healthcare provider is crucial to assess their specific risks and determine the appropriateness of a piercing.

Allergic Individuals:
Some individuals may have known allergies or sensitivities to certain metals or materials commonly used in piercing jewelry. Piercers should conduct a thorough allergy assessment and discuss alternative materials to ensure the client's safety and comfort. Using hypoallergenic or biocompatible materials, such as titanium or certain plastics, can help minimize the risk of allergic reactions.

In conclusion, special precautions and considerations are necessary when it comes to piercing specific groups of people. Whether it's pregnant individuals, children and minors, elderly individuals, those with medical conditions, immunocompromised individuals, or allergic individuals, piercers must adapt their practices to ensure the safety, well-being, and comfort of their clients. By understanding the unique risks and needs of these groups and seeking guidance from healthcare providers when necessary, piercers can provide a professional and safe piercing experience for everyone.

23.
Effects of Piercings on Physical and Mental Health

Piercings have become increasingly popular as a form of self-expression and body modification. While piercings can be visually appealing and culturally significant, it is essential to understand the potential effects they can have on both physical and mental health. In this chapter, we will explore the various aspects of how piercings can impact individuals' well-being.

Physical Effects:

Healing Process: When a piercing is performed, the body undergoes a healing process to accommodate the presence of jewelry. The healing time varies depending on the type of piercing and individual factors. During the healing process, individuals may experience tenderness, swelling, redness, and discharge around the piercing site. Proper aftercare, including cleaning and avoiding irritants, is crucial to promote healing and prevent complications such as infection.

Infection: One of the most common risks associated with piercings is infection. If proper hygiene practices are not followed, bacteria can enter the piercing site, leading to inflammation and infection. Symptoms of an infected piercing may include increased pain, redness, swelling, pus discharge, and fever. Prompt treatment with appropriate antibiotics is necessary to prevent the infection from spreading.

Allergic Reactions: Some individuals may experience allergic reactions to certain metals or materials used in piercing jewelry. Nickel, in particular, is a common allergen. Allergic reactions can manifest as itching, redness, swelling, and a rash around the piercing site. Using hypoallergenic jewelry, such as titanium or certain plastics, can help minimize the risk of allergic reactions.

Migration and Rejection: In some cases, the body may perceive the piercing as a foreign object and attempt to push it out. This can result in the migration or rejection of the jewelry, causing discomfort and potentially requiring the removal of the piercing. Factors such as improper placement, improper jewelry size or material, or individual body chemistry can contribute to migration or rejection.

Scarring: Scarring is a natural part of the healing process for piercings. While some scarring is expected, individuals may develop hypertrophic scars or keloids, which are raised, thickened scars that extend beyond the boundaries of the original piercing. Proper aftercare and avoiding trauma or excessive tension on the piercing can help minimize the risk of scarring.

Mental Health Effects:

Self-Expression and Identity: For many individuals, piercings serve as a means of self-expression, allowing them to showcase their personal style and identity. Piercings can boost self-confidence, promote self-acceptance, and enhance body positivity. They can be a form of artistic expression and a way to connect with a specific culture or community.

Body Image and Self-Esteem: The impact of piercings on body image and self-esteem can vary among individuals. While some may feel empowered and more confident with their piercings, others may experience self-consciousness or negative body image due to societal judgments or personal insecurities. It is crucial to consider individual perceptions and emotions when discussing the effects of piercings on mental health.

Psychological Well-Being: Piercings can also have psychological effects, such as a sense of empowerment, individuality, and personal satisfaction. Some individuals may find the piercing process cathartic or empowering, while others may experience increased self-awareness or a sense of personal growth. However, it is important to note that individual experiences may vary, and piercings should not be viewed as a substitute for addressing underlying mental health concerns.

Communication and Social Interactions: Piercings can influence interpersonal interactions and communication. They can serve as conversation starters, helping individuals connect with like-minded individuals or share their personal stories. However, piercings may also elicit judgment or discrimination from others, which can impact social interactions and relationships. It is essential to cultivate a supportive and accepting environment to foster positive social experiences.

Emotional and Psychological Challenges: Individuals may face emotional and psychological challenges during the piercing process, such as anxiety, fear, or stress. These feelings can stem from concerns about pain, potential complications, or the desire to meet societal expectations. Open communication, education about the process, and providing emotional support can help individuals navigate these challenges.

In conclusion, piercings can have both physical and mental health effects. While some physical effects, such as infection or migration, can pose risks and require proper care, piercings can also have positive impacts on self-expression, identity, and psychological well-being. Understanding the potential effects, practicing proper aftercare, and fostering open communication are essential for individuals and piercers to ensure a safe and positive piercing experience.

24.
Advanced Piercing Techniques and Procedures

Advanced piercing techniques and procedures are utilized by experienced piercers to create unique and intricate piercings. These techniques require a high level of skill, knowledge, and precision to ensure both the aesthetic appeal and the safety of the client. In this chapter, we will explore some of the advanced piercing techniques and procedures that are commonly performed by professional piercers.

Surface Piercings:
Surface piercings involve placing jewelry on flat or curved surfaces of the body, such as the nape of the neck, the collarbone, or the wrist. Unlike traditional piercings that go through a single entry and exit point, surface piercings require special considerations due to the unique anatomy of the area. Skilled piercers use flexible or surface-specific jewelry to minimize the risk of rejection or migration. Proper placement, appropriate jewelry selection, and meticulous aftercare are crucial for the successful healing of surface piercings.

Dermal Anchors:
Dermal anchors, also known as microdermal implants or single-point piercings, are a form of body modification where a small piece of jewelry is inserted into the dermal layer of the skin. This creates a decorative surface anchor point, allowing for the attachment of various types of jewelry. The procedure involves making a small incision in the skin, inserting the anchor, and securing it in place. Dermal anchors require advanced knowledge of anatomy, sterile technique, and precise placement to minimize complications and promote proper healing.

Genital Piercings:
Genital piercings encompass a wide range of piercings performed on the male or female genitalia. These piercings can be purely aesthetic or provide additional stimulation. Common genital piercings include Prince Albert, Christina, Labia, and Clitoral Hood piercings, among others. Genital piercings require a thorough understanding of the anatomy, proper jewelry selection, and meticulous aftercare due to the sensitive nature of the area. Skilled piercers must ensure open communication, informed consent, and a comfortable environment for clients seeking genital piercings.

Industrial Piercings:
Industrial piercings involve connecting two separate piercings on the ear cartilage using a single barbell or other jewelry. This creates a visually striking and unique piercing that spans the upper ear. The procedure requires precise placement, accurate measurement, and careful technique to ensure proper alignment and healing. Industrial piercings may take longer to heal and require additional aftercare due to the complexity of the piercing.

Oral Piercings:
Oral piercings refer to piercings done on the lips, tongue, or cheeks. These piercings include lip rings, labret piercings, tongue piercings, and cheek piercings. Oral piercings require specific knowledge of oral anatomy, the ability to work in a confined space, and a thorough understanding of the risks and complications associated with oral piercings. Proper placement, appropriate jewelry selection, and diligent aftercare are crucial for maintaining oral health and minimizing potential complications.

Scarification and Branding:
Scarification and branding are forms of body modification that involve intentional cutting, burning, or branding of the skin to create permanent designs. These procedures are highly specialized and require advanced knowledge, skill, and experience. Scarification and branding should only be performed by experienced professionals who have received appropriate training in these techniques. It is essential to prioritize client safety, informed consent, and strict adherence to sterile procedures when performing these advanced procedures.

In conclusion, advanced piercing techniques and procedures require a high level of skill, experience, and knowledge. Professional piercers who perform these advanced procedures must continuously update their skills, stay informed about industry advancements, and prioritize client safety and satisfaction. Clients seeking advanced piercings should research and select reputable piercers with a proven track record in performing these specialized techniques. Open communication, informed consent, and thorough aftercare are essential for successful outcomes and client satisfaction in advanced piercing procedures.

25.
Risks, Challenges, and Precautions for Advanced Piercing Techniques

Advanced piercing techniques offer individuals unique and personalized ways to express themselves through body modification. However, it's important to recognize that these techniques come with additional risks, challenges, and precautions that both piercers and clients should be aware of. In this chapter, we will explore the potential risks and challenges associated with advanced piercing techniques and discuss the necessary precautions to ensure a safe and successful experience.

Complex Anatomy and Placement:
Advanced piercing techniques often involve piercing areas with complex anatomy or unconventional placements. Piercers must have a thorough understanding of the anatomy of the specific area being pierced to avoid potential damage to nerves, blood vessels, or other vital structures. This requires advanced training, experience, and ongoing education to stay up-to-date with the latest anatomical knowledge.

Healing Challenges:
Piercings in challenging areas or with unique placements may present additional healing challenges. The body's natural healing process can be affected by factors such as increased movement, friction, or exposure to body fluids. Piercers must provide detailed aftercare instructions tailored to the specific piercing, including proper cleaning techniques, appropriate jewelry choices, and regular check-ups to monitor the healing progress.

Increased Risk of Infection:
With advanced piercing techniques, the risk of infection may be
higher due to the complexity of the piercing and the potential for
increased trauma during the procedure. It is crucial for piercers to
follow strict sterilization protocols, use single-use disposable needles
and sterile equipment, and educate clients about proper aftercare to
minimize the risk of infection. Regular monitoring and early detection
of any signs of infection are essential for prompt treatment.

Potential for Increased Pain:
Advanced piercings may be more painful compared to standard
piercings due to the nature of the procedure or the specific area being
pierced. It's important for piercers to manage client expectations and
provide appropriate pain management techniques, such as the use of
topical anesthetics or distraction techniques, to ensure a comfortable
and tolerable experience for the client.

Long-Term Maintenance and Jewelry Selection:
Advanced piercings often require specific types of jewelry that can
accommodate the unique placement or anatomy of the piercing.
Piercers must educate clients on the importance of selecting high-
quality jewelry made from suitable materials, such as implant-grade
titanium or solid gold, to minimize the risk of complications or
adverse reactions. Additionally, clients should be informed about the
need for regular jewelry downsizing or adjustments to ensure optimal
healing and long-term comfort.

Communication and Informed Consent:
Advanced piercing techniques may involve more extensive discussions
and consultations with clients to ensure they fully understand the risks,
challenges, and expected outcomes of the procedure. Piercers should
establish clear lines of communication, provide detailed information
about the procedure, and obtain informed consent from clients. This
includes discussing potential risks, complications, alternative options,
and realistic expectations to ensure the client is well-informed and
able to make an educated decision.

To mitigate these risks and overcome the challenges associated with advanced piercing techniques, piercers should prioritize ongoing education and professional development. They should stay updated on the latest techniques, industry standards, and best practices to ensure they provide the highest level of care and safety for their clients. Regular collaboration and consultation with other experienced piercers can also provide valuable insights and guidance in managing advanced piercing procedures.

In conclusion, advanced piercing techniques offer individuals unique and creative options for self-expression. However, it's important to approach these techniques with caution and to seek out skilled and experienced piercers who prioritize safety and adhere to best practices. By recognizing the potential risks and challenges, implementing appropriate precautions, and maintaining open communication with clients, piercers can help ensure a safe and successful experience for those seeking advanced piercings.

26.
Business Planning and Financial Management for Piercing Studios

Running a successful piercing studio requires not only technical expertise but also effective business planning and financial management. In this chapter, we will explore the key considerations and strategies for creating a solid business plan and managing the financial aspects of your piercing studio.

Business Plan Development:
A well-developed business plan serves as a roadmap for your piercing studio's success. It outlines your vision, mission, target market, competition analysis, marketing strategies, and financial projections. Your business plan should include information on your studio's unique selling points, pricing structure, services offered, and marketing tactics to attract and retain clients. It should also address potential challenges and provide strategies for growth and sustainability.

Location and Studio Setup:
Choosing the right location for your piercing studio is crucial for attracting clients and ensuring convenience and accessibility. Consider factors such as foot traffic, proximity to complementary businesses, and local zoning regulations. Additionally, invest in creating a comfortable and inviting studio space that reflects your brand and provides a safe and hygienic environment for clients.

Financial Management:
Managing your piercing studio's finances effectively is essential for long-term success. Create a comprehensive budget that includes all operational expenses, such as rent, utilities, supplies, licensing fees, insurance, marketing, and staff salaries. Monitor your cash flow regularly, track expenses and revenue, and make adjustments as needed to maintain a healthy financial position. Implementing an accounting system and working with a professional accountant can help you keep accurate financial records and make informed decisions.

Pricing Strategy:
Developing a competitive yet profitable pricing strategy is crucial for sustainable growth. Consider factors such as your target market, location, competition, and the value you provide to clients. Conduct market research to understand the average pricing in your area and adjust your prices accordingly. Find a balance between profitability and affordability to attract clients while ensuring your studio's financial viability.

Marketing and Branding:
Effective marketing and branding strategies are essential for attracting clients and building a loyal customer base. Develop a strong brand identity that aligns with your studio's values and target market. Utilize online and offline marketing channels to promote your services, such as creating a professional website, engaging in social media marketing, collaborating with local influencers, and participating in community events. Encourage positive reviews and testimonials from satisfied clients to build credibility and attract new customers.

Staff Management:

Your studio's success relies heavily on the expertise and professionalism of your staff. Hire skilled and knowledgeable piercers who are passionate about their craft and committed to providing excellent customer service. Implement ongoing training and professional development programs to enhance their skills and keep them updated with the latest trends and techniques. Foster a positive work environment that promotes teamwork, creativity, and a strong work ethic.

Customer Relationship Management:

Building strong relationships with your clients is crucial for repeat business and word-of-mouth referrals. Implement effective customer relationship management strategies, such as maintaining a client database, sending personalized follow-up emails or texts, offering loyalty programs, and seeking feedback to continually improve your services. Provide exceptional customer service by being responsive, attentive, and knowledgeable about aftercare and piercing-related concerns.

Growth and Expansion:

As your piercing studio grows, consider opportunities for expansion and diversification. This can include offering additional services, such as tattooing or body jewelry sales, opening additional locations, or introducing new products. Conduct market research, analyze industry trends, and evaluate the financial feasibility and demand for expansion options before making strategic decisions.

By implementing effective business planning and financial management strategies, you can establish a solid foundation for your piercing studio's success. Regularly review and update your business plan, monitor your financial performance, and adapt your strategies as needed to navigate challenges and seize opportunities. With a well-rounded approach to business management, you can create a thriving and profitable piercing studio that serves as a trusted destination for clients seeking professional and safe body modifications.

27.
Personnel Management and Staff Training

Personnel management plays a vital role in the overall success and smooth operation of a piercing studio. It involves various aspects such as recruitment, job descriptions, training, team communication, performance evaluation, conflict resolution, and staff retention. Let's delve into each of these areas in more detail:

Recruitment and Hiring:
The recruitment and hiring process is critical for finding the right individuals who will contribute to the success of your piercing studio. It is essential to identify candidates with relevant experience, knowledge, and skills in the piercing industry. Look for individuals who have a passion for the art of piercing and a strong commitment to providing excellent customer service. Conduct thorough interviews, check references, and assess their technical abilities to ensure they meet your studio's requirements.

Job Descriptions and Roles:
Creating clear and comprehensive job descriptions is essential for defining the roles and responsibilities of each staff member in your piercing studio. Outline the specific tasks and expectations for each position, including client consultations, piercing procedures, aftercare instructions, inventory management, and customer service. By establishing clear job descriptions, you set clear expectations for your staff and ensure they understand their roles within the studio.

Training and Development:
Investing in the training and development of your staff is crucial for their professional growth and the overall quality of service provided in your piercing studio. Develop a structured training program that covers both technical skills and customer service. This can include hands-on training, shadowing experienced staff members, and attending workshops or courses on topics such as infection control, jewelry selection, and aftercare procedures. Ongoing training and development opportunities help keep your staff up-to-date with industry trends, techniques, and best practices.

Team Communication and Collaboration:
Effective communication and collaboration among your staff members contribute to a positive and productive work environment. Encourage open dialogue, active listening, and respectful interactions among team members. Conduct regular staff meetings to provide a platform for discussions, sharing insights, and brainstorming ideas. Creating a culture of teamwork and collaboration fosters creativity, productivity, and job satisfaction among your staff.

Performance Evaluation and Feedback:
Regular performance evaluations are essential for assessing the strengths and areas for improvement of your staff members. Establish a feedback system that provides constructive criticism and recognition for their achievements. Set measurable goals and benchmarks to evaluate performance, and provide regular feedback on their progress. Recognize and reward outstanding performance to motivate and encourage your staff to continually improve their skills and contribute to the success of the studio.

Conflict Resolution:
Conflict can arise in any work environment, and it is crucial to address these issues promptly and effectively. Encourage open communication, active listening, and empathy when resolving conflicts. Implement a fair and transparent conflict resolution process that allows for constructive dialogue and finding mutually beneficial solutions. Addressing conflicts in a timely and respectful manner helps maintain a positive work environment and fosters strong team dynamics.

Staff Retention and Motivation:
Retaining skilled and motivated staff is key to the long-term success of your piercing studio. Implement strategies to recognize and reward your staff's contributions and achievements. Offer opportunities for career advancement and professional development within the studio. Foster a positive work environment that values work-life balance, supports staff well-being, and promotes a sense of belonging and fulfillment. By prioritizing staff retention and motivation, you can build a loyal and committed team.

In conclusion, effective personnel management and staff training are crucial for the success of a piercing studio. By recruiting the right individuals, defining clear job descriptions, providing comprehensive training and development opportunities, promoting teamwork and collaboration, conducting regular performance evaluations, addressing conflicts, and prioritizing staff retention and motivation, you can build a skilled and motivated team that delivers exceptional service to your clients.

28.
Marketing and Advertising for a Successful Piercing Studio

Marketing and advertising play a crucial role in the success of a piercing studio. Effective marketing strategies help attract new customers, build brand awareness, and establish a strong reputation in the industry. In this chapter, we will explore various marketing and advertising techniques that can be employed to ensure the success of a piercing studio.

Understanding the Target Market:
Before developing a marketing plan, it is important to understand the target market of the piercing studio. Identify the demographics, preferences, and behaviors of the target audience. This will help tailor marketing messages and campaigns to resonate with potential customers. Conduct market research, analyze customer feedback, and stay updated on industry trends to gain insights into the target market.

Branding and Identity:
Creating a strong brand identity is essential for a piercing studio to stand out in a competitive market. Develop a unique brand image that reflects the studio's values, personality, and aesthetic. This includes designing a compelling logo, selecting appropriate color schemes, and crafting a consistent brand voice. The brand identity should convey professionalism, creativity, and a commitment to safety and quality.

Online Presence:
In today's digital age, having a strong online presence is crucial for any business, including piercing studios. Develop a professional website that showcases the studio's services, portfolio, and aftercare instructions. Optimize the website for search engines to improve visibility. Establish a presence on social media platforms such as Facebook, Instagram, and Pinterest to engage with customers, share updates, and showcase the studio's work. Utilize online directories and review platforms to increase visibility and gather positive customer reviews.

Search Engine Optimization (SEO):
Implementing effective SEO strategies helps improve the visibility of a piercing studio's website in search engine results. Conduct keyword research to identify relevant search terms and incorporate them into website content, meta tags, and headings. Create informative and engaging content that appeals to both search engines and potential customers. Optimize the website's loading speed, mobile responsiveness, and user experience to improve search rankings.

Content Marketing:
Content marketing involves creating and sharing valuable and informative content to attract and engage potential customers. Develop a blog section on the website where educational articles, piercing trends, and aftercare tips can be shared. Create video tutorials, infographics, and visual content to engage with the audience on social media platforms. This helps establish the studio as a trusted source of information and builds credibility and trust with potential customers.

Community Engagement:
Engaging with the local community is an effective way to build awareness and attract customers to a piercing studio. Sponsor local events, collaborate with other businesses, and participate in community activities. Offer discounts or promotions to local residents or organize workshops and informational sessions about piercing safety and aftercare. This helps establish the studio as a reputable and trusted entity within the community.

Word-of-Mouth Marketing:
Word-of-mouth marketing is a powerful tool for a piercing studio. Encourage satisfied customers to spread the word about their positive experiences. Offer referral incentives to existing customers who refer new clients. Showcase customer testimonials and before-and-after photos on the website and social media platforms. Providing exceptional customer service and a memorable experience will naturally generate positive word-of-mouth referrals.

Paid Advertising:

Consider utilizing paid advertising channels to reach a wider audience. This may include online advertising platforms like Google Ads, social media ads, or sponsored content on relevant websites or blogs. Set clear goals and budgets for paid advertising campaigns and monitor their performance regularly. Test different ad formats, targeting options, and messaging to optimize the return on investment.

In conclusion, effective marketing and advertising strategies are essential for the success of a piercing studio. By understanding the target market, developing a strong brand identity, establishing a strong online presence, implementing SEO techniques, creating valuable content, engaging with the community, utilizing word-of-mouth marketing, and considering paid advertising options, a piercing studio can attract new customers, build brand awareness, and foster a loyal customer base.

29.
Ethical Considerations in the Context of Piercing

Ethics play a crucial role in the field of piercing, as it involves making decisions that prioritize the well-being and autonomy of clients. Piercers must adhere to a set of ethical considerations to ensure a safe and respectful environment for their clients. In this chapter, we will explore the key ethical considerations that piercers should take into account.

Informed Consent:
One of the fundamental ethical principles in piercing is obtaining informed consent from clients. This means providing comprehensive information about the piercing procedure, potential risks and complications, aftercare instructions, and the expected healing process. Piercers should ensure that clients have a clear understanding of the procedure and actively consent to it before proceeding. It is important to address any questions or concerns raised by clients and respect their autonomy in making decisions about their own bodies.

Client Confidentiality:
Respecting client confidentiality is essential in maintaining trust and privacy. Piercers should ensure that all client information, including personal details, medical history, and piercing records, are kept confidential and only shared with the client's explicit consent. This includes storing physical and electronic records securely and following data protection regulations. Respecting client confidentiality helps create a safe space where clients can feel comfortable sharing personal information without fear of judgment or unauthorized disclosure.

Hygiene and Sterilization:
Maintaining a high standard of hygiene and sterilization is both an ethical and a safety consideration. Piercers have a responsibility to follow strict hygiene practices, such as wearing gloves, using sterile equipment, and properly disinfecting the piercing area. Adhering to these practices minimizes the risk of infections and ensures the well-being of clients. Piercers should also educate clients on proper aftercare practices to promote hygiene and prevent complications.

Respecting Cultural and Personal Values:
Piercers should be sensitive to cultural, religious, and personal values when providing piercing services. This includes understanding and respecting any cultural or religious restrictions regarding specific piercings. Piercers should also consider individual preferences and provide a supportive and non-judgmental environment. Respecting cultural and personal values demonstrates inclusivity and helps foster a positive and respectful client-piercer relationship.

Continuing Education and Professionalism:
Ethical piercers prioritize ongoing education and professional development. Staying up-to-date with the latest techniques, safety guidelines, and industry trends is essential for providing the best possible care to clients. Piercers should actively seek opportunities for training, attend workshops and conferences, and engage in peer discussions. By continuously improving their skills and knowledge, piercers can enhance the quality of their services and maintain professionalism.

Conflict of Interest:
Piercers must avoid conflicts of interest that may compromise their professional judgment. This includes refraining from promoting unnecessary piercings or recommending specific jewelry solely for financial gain. Piercers should prioritize the best interests and well-being of their clients and provide honest and unbiased advice. Maintaining transparency and integrity in all interactions with clients helps build trust and ensures ethical practice.

Collaboration and Referrals:
In some cases, piercers may encounter situations that fall outside their expertise or require specialized medical attention. In such instances, it is important to collaborate with healthcare professionals and refer clients to appropriate specialists. This demonstrates a commitment to the client's well-being and ensures that they receive the necessary care and support.

By embracing these ethical considerations, piercers can establish a foundation of trust, respect, and professionalism in their practice. Ethical practice not only benefits clients but also contributes to the overall reputation and advancement of the piercing industry. It is important for piercers to continually reflect on their ethical responsibilities and make informed decisions that prioritize the health, safety, and autonomy of their clients.

30.
Respecting Customer Rights and Privacy

Respecting customer rights and privacy is of utmost importance in a piercing studio. It goes beyond simply providing quality services and encompasses creating a safe, comfortable, and respectful environment for clients. In this chapter, we will delve into the various aspects of respecting customer rights and privacy in a piercing studio and explore how piercers can go above and beyond to ensure a positive and ethical experience for their clients.

Confidentiality and Data Protection:

One of the primary responsibilities of piercers is to maintain the confidentiality of client information and protect their personal data. This includes implementing stringent measures to safeguard client records and sensitive information. Piercers should establish clear protocols for data storage, ensuring that client information is securely stored, accessed only by authorized personnel, and protected from unauthorized disclosure. Adhering to data protection regulations and utilizing encryption technologies when necessary can further enhance the security of client information.

Informed Consent:

Respecting customer rights means obtaining informed consent from clients before performing any piercing procedure. It is essential to provide clients with comprehensive information about the procedure, including the potential risks, benefits, and aftercare requirements. Piercers should take the time to educate clients on the specific piercing they are interested in, discuss any potential complications, and answer any questions or concerns they may have. By ensuring that clients are well-informed, piercers empower them to make decisions based on their individual preferences and needs.

Respecting Autonomy and Choice:

Every individual has the right to make decisions about their own body, including whether to get a piercing and what type of piercing to get. Respecting customer rights means honoring and supporting clients' autonomy and choices. Piercers should avoid imposing their personal opinions or preferences on clients and instead provide unbiased information and guidance. It is essential to create a non-judgmental and inclusive environment where clients feel comfortable expressing their preferences and making choices that align with their values and personal style.

Privacy during Procedures:

During the actual piercing procedure, respecting customer privacy is paramount. Piercers should take appropriate measures to ensure that clients feel comfortable and their privacy is protected. This may include providing private rooms or curtained areas where clients can change or prepare for the procedure, using drapes or barriers to shield sensitive areas, and maintaining a professional and respectful demeanor throughout the process. Respecting privacy helps to create a sense of trust and comfort for clients, enhancing their overall experience.

Handling Personal Information:

Piercing studios must handle personal information with the utmost care and responsibility. This includes collecting only necessary information from clients, securely storing their records, and implementing protocols for the safe handling and disposal of personal data. Piercers should educate themselves about data protection regulations and best practices to ensure compliance and the highest level of security for client information. Additionally, piercers should be mindful of how they communicate with clients, ensuring that sensitive information is not shared inappropriately or overheard by others.

Conflict Resolution:

Respecting customer rights involves establishing effective mechanisms for resolving conflicts or addressing concerns that may arise during the piercing process. Piercers should have clear communication channels in place and be prepared to listen actively to client feedback and complaints. It is important to approach conflicts with empathy, patience, and a willingness to find a mutually satisfactory resolution. Resolving conflicts in a fair and transparent manner not only demonstrates respect for customer rights but also helps to maintain a positive and long-lasting relationship with clients.

Continuing Education and Professional Development:

To continuously improve in respecting customer rights and privacy, piercers should prioritize ongoing education and professional development. This includes staying updated on relevant laws and regulations related to privacy and data protection, attending workshops or seminars on ethical practices, and seeking out opportunities to enhance their knowledge and skills in this area. By investing in continuous learning, piercers can ensure that they are upholding the highest ethical standards and providing the best possible experience for their clients.

In conclusion, respecting customer rights and privacy is a fundamental aspect of operating a professional and ethical piercing studio. By prioritizing confidentiality, obtaining informed consent, respecting autonomy and choice, ensuring privacy during procedures, handling personal information responsibly, addressing conflicts with empathy, and investing in continuous education, piercers can create a safe and respectful environment that upholds the rights and privacy of their clients.

31.
Responsible Handling of Piercing Jewelry, Materials, and Waste Disposal

Proper handling of piercing jewelry, materials, and waste disposal is essential for maintaining a safe and hygienic environment in a piercing studio. In this chapter, we will explore the importance of responsible handling practices and provide guidelines for the appropriate disposal of piercing-related waste.

Handling Piercing Jewelry and Materials:
When it comes to piercing jewelry and materials, it is crucial to prioritize cleanliness and sterility. Here are some key considerations:

Sterilization and Sanitization: All piercing jewelry and equipment should undergo proper sterilization or sanitization procedures before use. This involves using autoclaves, ultrasonic cleaners, or chemical solutions to eliminate any potential pathogens or contaminants.

Storage and Organization: Piercing jewelry and materials should be stored in clean and well-organized containers to prevent cross-contamination. Each type of jewelry should be clearly labeled and separated to ensure easy access and minimize the risk of mix-ups.

Disposable vs. Reusable: Some piercing jewelry, such as needles, should always be single-use and disposable to prevent the transmission of infections. Other items, like forceps or clamps, can be reusable but require thorough cleaning and sterilization after each use.

Regular Inspections: Regular inspections of piercing jewelry and materials are necessary to ensure their integrity and effectiveness. Any damaged or worn-out items should be promptly replaced to maintain the highest standards of safety and quality.

Waste Disposal:
Proper disposal of piercing-related waste is essential to prevent contamination and protect the environment. Here are some guidelines for responsible waste disposal:

Biohazard Waste: Any waste that comes into contact with blood or bodily fluids, such as used needles or contaminated dressings, should be considered biohazard waste. This waste should be placed in designated biohazard containers and disposed of according to local regulations and guidelines.

Sharps Disposal: Used needles, lancets, or any other sharp objects should be discarded in puncture-proof containers specifically designed for sharps disposal. These containers should be securely sealed and labeled to prevent accidental injuries.

General Waste: Non-contaminated waste, such as packaging materials or disposable gloves, can be disposed of in regular trash bins. However, it is important to separate recyclable materials whenever possible to minimize environmental impact.

Chemical Waste: Some piercing-related materials, such as cleaning solutions or disinfectants, may be considered hazardous waste. These substances should be handled and disposed of according to local regulations and guidelines. It is essential to consult with appropriate authorities or waste management services to ensure proper disposal methods.

Environmental Responsibility:
In addition to proper waste disposal, piercers should also consider their environmental impact and strive to minimize it. Here are some practices to promote environmental responsibility:

Reduce, Reuse, Recycle: Implement recycling programs within the studio to encourage the proper disposal of recyclable materials. Additionally, consider ways to reduce waste generation and opt for reusable items whenever possible.

Sustainable Materials: Choose piercing jewelry and materials made from sustainable and environmentally friendly materials, such as recycled metals or biodegradable options. This demonstrates a commitment to sustainability and reduces the reliance on non-renewable resources.

Education and Awareness: Educate staff and clients about the importance of responsible waste disposal and environmental sustainability. Provide information on recycling options, proper disposal methods, and the studio's efforts to reduce its environmental footprint.

By adhering to responsible handling practices and implementing proper waste disposal procedures, piercing studios can create a safe and environmentally conscious environment. Prioritizing cleanliness, sterility, and the appropriate disposal of waste demonstrates professionalism, care for clients' well-being, and a commitment to environmental stewardship.

32.
Emergency Measures and First Aid in the Piercing Studio

In a piercing studio, it is important to be prepared for emergencies and have the necessary knowledge and skills to provide immediate first aid. This chapter focuses on the emergency measures and first aid techniques that piercers should be familiar with to ensure the safety and well-being of their clients.

Emergency Preparedness:
Having a well-equipped first aid kit readily available in the piercing studio is essential. The first aid kit should include items such as gloves, sterile dressings, adhesive bandages, antiseptic solutions, scissors, and a CPR mask. Additionally, piercers should be trained in basic life support techniques, including cardiopulmonary resuscitation (CPR) and the use of an automated external defibrillator (AED).

Assessment and Communication:
In the event of an emergency, piercers should quickly assess the situation and communicate with the client and any other individuals involved. This includes identifying any immediate dangers, assessing the client's condition, and determining the appropriate course of action. Clear communication with the client, as well as contacting emergency services if necessary, is crucial for ensuring timely and appropriate medical assistance.

Bleeding and Wound Care:
Piercings can sometimes result in bleeding or minor injuries. Piercers should be skilled in controlling bleeding by applying direct pressure to the wound using sterile dressings or clean materials. They should also know how to clean and dress wounds properly to prevent infection. Additionally, piercers should be able to recognize signs of excessive bleeding or more severe injuries that may require immediate medical attention.

Allergic Reactions and Anaphylaxis:
While rare, allergic reactions to piercing materials or jewelry can occur. Piercers should be able to recognize the signs and symptoms of an allergic reaction, such as itching, redness, swelling, or difficulty breathing. In severe cases, anaphylaxis, a life-threatening allergic reaction, may occur. Piercers should know how to administer emergency medications, such as epinephrine, and be familiar with the steps for managing anaphylaxis until medical help arrives.

Infections and Abscesses:
Infections can occur in piercings if proper aftercare is not followed. Piercers should be knowledgeable about the signs of infection, such as increased redness, swelling, warmth, or discharge. They should advise clients on proper aftercare practices and provide guidance on recognizing and managing infections. In cases where an abscess forms, piercers should refer clients to medical professionals for appropriate treatment.

Shock and Fainting:
In some situations, clients may experience shock or fainting. Piercers should be able to recognize the signs and symptoms of shock, such as pale skin, rapid breathing, or a weak pulse. They should know how to position the client to help alleviate symptoms and provide reassurance and support. In cases of fainting, piercers should ensure the client is in a safe position and monitor their vital signs until they recover.

Documentation and Follow-up:
Following any emergency or first aid intervention, it is important to document the incident, including the actions taken and any relevant information. This documentation helps in maintaining a record of the incident, enables follow-up care, and may be required for legal or insurance purposes. Additionally, piercers should provide appropriate aftercare instructions and follow up with clients to ensure their well-being and address any concerns.

Regular Training and Updating:
To ensure proficiency in emergency measures and first aid, piercers should regularly undergo training and stay updated on the latest techniques and guidelines. This includes attending first aid and CPR courses, participating in workshops or seminars on emergency response, and staying informed about best practices in first aid. Regular training helps piercers maintain their skills and knowledge, enabling them to respond effectively in emergency situations.

In conclusion, being prepared for emergencies and having the ability to provide first aid is crucial in a piercing studio. By having a well-equipped first aid kit, being trained in emergency response techniques, and knowing how to assess and address common emergencies, piercers can ensure the safety and well-being of their clients. Regular training and staying updated on first aid practices contribute to a safe and professional environment in the piercing studio.

33.
Dealing with Emergencies and Crisis Situations in Piercing

Introduction:
In the piercing industry, it is crucial for piercers to be prepared to handle emergencies and crisis situations that may arise during the piercing process. Being equipped with the knowledge, skills, and resources to respond effectively can make a significant difference in ensuring the safety and well-being of both the piercer and the client. In this chapter, we will explore various aspects of dealing with emergencies and crisis situations in piercing.

Prevention and Risk Assessment:
Prevention is always the best approach when it comes to emergencies. Piercers should prioritize the implementation of preventive measures to minimize the risk of accidents or complications. This includes thorough risk assessments before performing any piercing procedure, checking for any pre-existing health conditions or allergies, and ensuring the cleanliness and sterility of the studio environment and equipment. By identifying and addressing potential risks, piercers can proactively reduce the likelihood of emergencies occurring.

Emergency Preparedness:
Having a well-defined emergency plan is essential for handling crisis situations effectively. Piercers should establish protocols and procedures for different emergency scenarios, such as severe allergic reactions, excessive bleeding, or fainting. This plan should include clear instructions on how to assess the situation, when to seek medical assistance, and how to provide immediate care until professional help arrives. Regular training and practice sessions can help piercers and their staff develop the necessary skills and confidence to respond calmly and efficiently during emergencies.

Emergency Equipment and Supplies:
A properly stocked and easily accessible emergency kit is a critical component of emergency preparedness in a piercing studio. The kit should include essential items such as sterile gauze pads, bandages, antiseptic solutions, disposable gloves, and emergency contact information. Additionally, having tools like a CPR mask, an automated external defibrillator (AED), and a first aid manual can greatly enhance the ability to provide immediate care during critical situations. It is essential to regularly check the expiration dates of supplies and replace them as needed.

Communication and Crisis Management:
Clear and effective communication is paramount during emergencies and crisis situations. Piercers should establish a system for notifying staff members and clients in the event of an emergency, ensuring that everyone is aware of their roles and responsibilities. Providing reassurance and clear instructions to the affected individuals can help maintain a calm atmosphere and facilitate the necessary actions. Additionally, maintaining open lines of communication with emergency medical services and other relevant authorities is crucial for timely and coordinated responses.

Post-Emergency Care and Support:
Once an emergency situation has been successfully managed, it is important to provide appropriate follow-up care and support to the affected individual. This may include monitoring their condition, offering guidance on aftercare, and providing resources for any necessary medical follow-up. Additionally, offering emotional support and addressing any concerns or questions the client may have can contribute to their overall well-being and recovery process. Keeping accurate and detailed records of the emergency incident and the steps taken can also be valuable for future reference and learning.

Continuous Training and Improvement:
The piercing industry is constantly evolving, and it is essential for piercers to stay updated with the latest knowledge and techniques in emergency response and crisis management. Continuous training, attending relevant workshops or seminars, and seeking professional certifications in first aid and emergency care can enhance the skills and preparedness of piercers. Regularly reviewing and updating emergency protocols based on feedback and lessons learned from past incidents is crucial for continuous improvement and ensuring the highest standard of safety and care.

Conclusion:
Dealing with emergencies and crisis situations requires thorough preparation, effective communication, and the ability to respond calmly and confidently. By implementing preventive measures, establishing emergency protocols, maintaining well-equipped emergency kits, and continuously updating their knowledge and skills, piercers can create a safe environment for both themselves and their clients. It is crucial to prioritize the safety and well-being of everyone involved, and by doing so, piercers can confidently handle emergencies and crisis situations in the piercing industry.

34.
Continuing Education and Professional Development as a Piercer

As a piercer, it is essential to recognize the importance of continuing education and professional development in order to stay current with industry trends, advancements, and best practices. The field of piercing is constantly evolving, and it is crucial to invest time and effort into furthering your knowledge and skills. In this chapter, we will explore the benefits of continuing education and professional development for piercers and provide strategies for ongoing learning and growth.

Benefits of Continuing Education:

Stay Updated with Industry Trends: Continuing education allows piercers to stay informed about the latest trends, techniques, and materials in the field. This knowledge can help you provide innovative and up-to-date services to your clients, keeping your studio at the forefront of the industry.

Enhance Technical Skills: Ongoing training and workshops provide opportunities to refine and expand your technical skills as a piercer. From mastering advanced piercing techniques to learning about new tools and equipment, continuing education helps you deliver high-quality services to your clients.

Professional Growth and Recognition: By investing in your professional development, you demonstrate your commitment to excellence and continuous improvement. This can lead to increased recognition within the industry, building your reputation as a skilled and knowledgeable piercer.

Networking Opportunities: Continuing education events, conferences, and workshops offer valuable networking opportunities. Engaging with fellow piercers, industry experts, and suppliers can foster relationships, provide mentorship, and open doors to collaboration and growth.

Strategies for Ongoing Learning and Growth:

Attend Industry Conferences and Workshops: Make it a priority to attend industry conferences and workshops to expand your knowledge and skills. These events often feature presentations, demonstrations, and hands-on training sessions conducted by experienced professionals in the field.

Engage in Online Learning: Take advantage of online platforms, webinars, and courses dedicated to piercing and body modification. These resources offer flexibility in terms of scheduling and allow you to learn at your own pace.

Seek Mentorship: Connect with experienced piercers who can serve as mentors and provide guidance on various aspects of the profession. Mentorship relationships can offer valuable insights, advice, and support throughout your career.

Participate in Professional Associations: Joining professional piercing associations and organizations provides access to resources, industry updates, and networking opportunities. These associations often offer educational materials, forums for discussion, and certification programs.

Stay Informed through Publications: Subscribe to industry magazines, journals, and online publications to stay informed about the latest developments and research in piercing. These publications often feature articles written by experts, case studies, and interviews with industry leaders.

Collaborate with Other Professionals: Collaborate with professionals from related fields, such as dermatologists, healthcare providers, or jewelry designers. This collaboration can broaden your perspective, enhance your knowledge, and lead to innovative approaches in piercing.

Pursue Specialty Certifications: Consider pursuing specialty certifications in specific areas of piercing, such as genital piercing or dermal anchoring. These certifications demonstrate your expertise and can attract a niche clientele.

Continuing education and professional development are essential for piercers who strive for excellence and want to provide the best possible services to their clients. By staying updated with industry trends, enhancing technical skills, networking with peers, and engaging in ongoing learning, you can continue to grow as a piercer and contribute to the advancement of the field.

35.
Networking and Collaboration with Other Piercers and Industry Professionals

Networking and collaboration with other piercers and industry professionals is a valuable aspect of professional growth and development in the piercing industry. By building connections and fostering relationships with peers, you can expand your knowledge, gain new perspectives, and open doors to exciting opportunities. In this chapter, we will explore the importance of networking and collaboration and provide strategies for effective engagement.

Networking with other piercers and industry professionals allows you to tap into a vast pool of knowledge and expertise. Attending industry events such as conferences, conventions, and workshops provides an excellent opportunity to meet fellow piercers, share experiences, and learn from each other. Engage in conversations, participate in panel discussions, and take advantage of networking sessions to connect with like-minded professionals who share your passion for piercing.

Online communities and forums dedicated to the piercing industry can also be valuable networking platforms. Joining these communities allows you to engage in discussions, ask questions, and seek advice from experienced piercers around the world. Take an active role in contributing to the community by sharing your own knowledge and experiences, and be open to learning from others.

Collaboration with other piercers and industry professionals can lead to exciting opportunities for growth and exposure. Consider partnering with other piercers to organize workshops or educational events where you can share your expertise with a wider audience. Collaborative projects such as photo shoots, publications, or research studies can also showcase your skills and enhance your professional reputation.

Building a strong network of contacts can also lead to referrals and collaborations with other professionals in related fields. Establishing relationships with tattoo artists, jewelry manufacturers, dermatologists, or healthcare professionals can create a network of resources and potential partnerships. These collaborations can provide valuable insights, enhance your services, and expand your client base.

When networking and collaborating, it is important to approach interactions with professionalism and respect. Be open-minded and willing to learn from others, and be generous in sharing your own knowledge and experiences. Actively listen to others, ask thoughtful questions, and show genuine interest in their work. Remember that networking is a two-way street, and building relationships requires nurturing and reciprocity.

To maximize the benefits of networking and collaboration, it is essential to maintain ongoing communication and follow-up with your contacts. Connect with them on social media platforms, exchange contact information, and stay in touch through email or occasional meetings. By nurturing these relationships, you can stay informed about industry trends, upcoming events, and potential opportunities for collaboration.

Networking and collaboration go beyond professional growth—they can also contribute to a sense of community and support within the industry. By fostering connections with fellow piercers and industry professionals, you can create a support system where you can share challenges, seek advice, and celebrate successes together. This sense of camaraderie can be invaluable in navigating the ups and downs of the piercing industry.

In summary, networking and collaboration with other piercers and industry professionals are essential for professional growth and development in the piercing industry. Engage in networking opportunities through industry events, online communities, and collaborations. Approach interactions with professionalism, respect, and a willingness to learn from others. Nurture relationships by maintaining ongoing communication and follow-up. By building a strong network of contacts, you can expand your knowledge, explore new opportunities, and foster a sense of community within the industry.

36.
Current Trends and Developments in the Field of Body Piercing

Body piercing is an ever-evolving industry, influenced by changing fashion trends, cultural shifts, and advancements in piercing techniques and technology. In this chapter, we will explore some of the current trends and developments that are shaping the world of body piercing.

Minimalist and Delicate Designs:
In recent years, there has been a growing trend towards minimalist and delicate designs in body piercing. Instead of large and bold jewelry, many people are opting for smaller, dainty pieces that complement their individual style. This trend is especially popular in ear piercings, with multiple earlobe piercings and delicate helix or tragus piercings becoming increasingly common.

Multiple Piercings and Ear Stacking:
Another prominent trend in body piercing is the concept of multiple piercings and ear stacking. People are embracing the opportunity to create unique and personalized combinations of piercings on their ears, creating intricate patterns and arrangements. This trend allows individuals to express their individuality and create a look that is completely their own.

Surface and Dermal Piercings:
Surface and dermal piercings are gaining popularity as people seek more unique and unconventional piercing placements. Surface piercings involve placing jewelry on the surface of the skin, while dermal piercings, also known as microdermal or single-point piercings, involve inserting an anchor under the skin and attaching jewelry to it. These types of piercings offer endless possibilities for creativity and self-expression.

Mixed Metals and Custom Jewelry:
The use of mixed metals and custom jewelry is a growing trend in body piercing. People are no longer limited to traditional materials like stainless steel or titanium. Instead, they are exploring a wide range of materials, including gold, rose gold, and even precious gemstones. Custom jewelry allows individuals to create unique pieces that reflect their personal style and preferences.

Advanced Piercing Techniques:
Advancements in piercing techniques and technology have opened up new possibilities in the field of body piercing. Piercers are now able to offer procedures such as surface anchors, microdermals, and even more complex genital piercings with improved precision and safety. These advancements have expanded the options available to individuals seeking unique and specialized piercings.

Emphasis on Safety and Sterilization:
As body piercing continues to gain popularity, there is an increasing emphasis on safety and sterilization practices. Piercers are adopting stricter standards and protocols to ensure the well-being of their clients. This includes the use of single-use, sterile needles and jewelry, adherence to strict sterilization procedures, and ongoing education on infection control and safety practices.

Inclusive and Diverse Representation:
In recent years, there has been a push for greater inclusivity and diversity within the body piercing industry. People from all walks of life are seeking piercings to express their identities and individuality. As a result, piercers are becoming more aware of the importance of offering a welcoming and inclusive environment for clients of all backgrounds and identities.

Holistic Approaches to Aftercare:
In addition to the actual piercing process, there is a growing focus on
holistic approaches to aftercare. Piercers are providing clients with
comprehensive information and guidance on how to care for their
piercings, including proper cleaning methods, appropriate products,
and lifestyle considerations. This holistic approach takes into account
not only the physical aspects of healing but also the emotional and
mental well-being of clients.

Sustainability and Eco-Friendly Practices:
The body piercing industry is also experiencing a shift towards
sustainability and eco-friendly practices. Piercers are opting for
environmentally friendly packaging, using recyclable materials, and
sourcing jewelry from ethical suppliers. This commitment to
sustainability aligns with the broader movement towards conscious
consumerism and responsible business practices.

Continuing Education and Professional Development:
As the field of body piercing evolves, there is a growing recognition of
the importance of continuing education and professional development
for piercers. Keeping up with the latest techniques, safety protocols,
and industry trends is crucial for providing clients with the best
possible service. Piercers are attending conferences, workshops, and
seminars, and actively seeking out opportunities to expand their
knowledge and skills.

In conclusion, the field of body piercing is constantly evolving, driven
by current trends, technological advancements, and changing
consumer preferences. The trends and developments discussed in this
chapter provide a glimpse into the exciting and diverse world of body
piercing. Whether it's minimalist designs, advanced techniques, or a
focus on sustainability, the industry continues to push boundaries and
offer new possibilities for self-expression and individuality.

37.
Technological Advancements and their Impact on Piercing

Technological advancements have had a significant impact on the field of piercing, revolutionizing the way piercers perform procedures and enhancing the overall piercing experience for clients. In this chapter, we will explore some of the key technological advancements and their effects on the piercing industry.

Improved Piercing Techniques:
Technological advancements have led to the development of more advanced and precise piercing techniques. For example, the introduction of specialized piercing needles, such as cannula needles or beveled needles, has made the piercing process smoother and less painful for clients. These needles allow for more precise control and minimize tissue trauma, resulting in faster healing and improved outcomes.

Sterilization and Safety Equipment:
Technological advancements have greatly improved sterilization and safety practices in piercing studios. Autoclaves, for example, have become more advanced, allowing for efficient and effective sterilization of piercing tools and equipment. Additionally, digital sterilization monitoring systems provide real-time feedback on the sterilization process, ensuring that all instruments meet the required safety standards.

Advanced Piercing Tools and Jewelry:
Technological innovations have led to the development of new piercing tools and jewelry materials. For instance, the use of disposable piercing needles has become more prevalent, eliminating the risk of cross-contamination between clients. Additionally, the introduction of high-quality, hypoallergenic materials like implant-grade titanium or niobium has allowed for safer and more comfortable piercings.

Digital Design and Visualization:
Advancements in digital design and visualization technology have revolutionized the way piercers plan and execute piercings. Computer-aided design (CAD) software allows piercers to create accurate and detailed designs, taking into account factors such as anatomical variations and client preferences. Virtual reality (VR) and augmented reality (AR) technologies enable clients to visualize their desired piercings before the procedure, ensuring a clearer understanding of the final result.

Online Presence and E-commerce:
The rise of the internet and e-commerce has had a profound impact on the piercing industry. Piercers can now showcase their work and reach a wider audience through websites and social media platforms. Clients have the convenience of browsing through portfolios, reading reviews, and scheduling appointments online. E-commerce platforms also allow for the easy purchase of jewelry and aftercare products, expanding access and choice for clients.

Remote Consultations and Aftercare Support:
Technological advancements have enabled piercers to offer remote consultations and aftercare support to clients. Video conferencing platforms allow for virtual consultations, where clients can discuss their piercing goals and receive professional advice without being physically present. Additionally, digital platforms and mobile applications provide clients with personalized aftercare instructions and reminders, ensuring proper healing and reducing the risk of complications.

Data Management and Client Records:
Technology has streamlined data management and client record-keeping in piercing studios. Electronic health records (EHR) systems enable piercers to securely store and access client information, including piercing history, aftercare instructions, and allergies. This digitalization improves efficiency, organization, and accessibility, ensuring that piercers can provide personalized and informed care to their clients.

In conclusion, technological advancements have significantly influenced the field of piercing, enhancing safety, precision, and client satisfaction. Improved piercing techniques, advanced sterilization equipment, digital design tools, and online platforms have revolutionized the way piercers operate and interact with clients. By embracing these technological advancements, piercers can provide a higher level of service, ensure better outcomes, and adapt to the changing needs and expectations of clients in the modern era.

38.
Personal Perspectives and Future Plans as a Piercer

Being a piercer is not just a profession but a passion for many individuals. In this chapter, we will explore the personal perspectives and future plans of piercers, shedding light on their motivations, aspirations, and visions for their careers in the piercing industry.

For many piercers, their journey in the industry started as a personal interest or fascination with body modification. They were drawn to the artistry and the ability to help individuals express their identities through piercing. This personal connection to the craft fuels their dedication and commitment to providing high-quality and safe piercing experiences for their clients.

One common perspective among piercers is the importance of continuous learning and professional development. They understand that the industry is constantly evolving, and staying up to date with the latest techniques, trends, and safety protocols is crucial. Piercers actively seek out educational opportunities, attend workshops and conferences, and engage in mentorship programs to expand their knowledge and skills. They embrace the idea that learning is a lifelong process and strive to be at the forefront of their field.

The personal satisfaction derived from the positive impact they have on their clients' lives is a driving force for many piercers. They take pride in helping individuals overcome fears, boost their confidence, and enhance their self-expression through piercings. The joy of witnessing their clients' transformation and the gratitude they receive fuels their passion and drives them to provide exceptional services.

In terms of future plans, piercers have diverse aspirations and goals. Some envision opening their own piercing studios, where they can create a safe and welcoming environment for clients and cultivate their own artistic vision. They strive to build a reputation for excellence and innovation, attracting a loyal clientele and establishing themselves as leaders in the industry.

Others aspire to contribute to the field of piercing through education and mentorship. They aim to share their knowledge and experience with aspiring piercers, guiding them in their journey and ensuring the industry's continued growth and professionalism. They may envision teaching workshops, writing books, or developing online resources to disseminate valuable information and promote best practices.

Moreover, piercers recognize the importance of community and collaboration within the industry. They value the support and knowledge-sharing that comes from connecting with other piercers and industry professionals. They actively participate in professional networks, attend industry events, and engage in collaborative projects. They understand that by working together, they can elevate the standards of the industry and foster a sense of unity and camaraderie.

As the piercing industry continues to evolve, piercers are aware of the need to adapt to changing trends, advancements in technology, and evolving customer preferences. They embrace innovation and are open to exploring new techniques, materials, and styles to meet the ever-growing demands of their clients. They understand the importance of embracing diversity, inclusivity, and cultural sensitivity to provide a personalized and inclusive experience for all clients.

In conclusion, being a piercer is not just a job but a lifelong passion for many individuals. Their personal perspectives, dedication to continuous learning, and aspirations for the future shape their careers in the piercing industry. Whether it's opening their own studio, contributing to education and mentorship, or fostering collaboration within the industry, piercers are driven by their love for the craft and the desire to make a positive impact on the lives of their clients.

39.
Conclusion

In conclusion, the world of body piercing is a dynamic and diverse industry that continues to evolve and thrive. Throughout this book, we have explored various aspects of piercing, from its history and cultural significance to the technical skills required and the ethical considerations involved.

Piercing is not just a form of body modification; it is an art form that allows individuals to express their identity, creativity, and personal style. From the minimalist designs to the intricate arrangements, people are embracing the endless possibilities that piercing offers.

One of the key themes that emerged from our discussions is the importance of safety, hygiene, and professionalism in the piercing industry. Piercers are committed to providing a safe and comfortable environment for their clients, adhering to strict sterilization procedures, and staying updated on the latest industry standards and practices. The well-being of their clients is always their top priority.

Another significant aspect we explored is the role of communication and education. Piercers understand the importance of building a strong rapport with their clients, listening to their needs and preferences, and providing them with comprehensive information and aftercare instructions. They also prioritize their own professional development, continuously seeking opportunities to expand their knowledge and refine their skills.

Furthermore, we discussed the importance of maintaining ethical practices in the field of piercing. Respecting client rights and privacy, promoting inclusivity and diversity, and embracing sustainable and eco-friendly approaches are integral to the ethical framework of the industry.

As we look to the future, we anticipate further advancements in piercing techniques, jewelry designs, and industry standards. Piercers will continue to adapt and innovate to meet the evolving needs and desires of their clients.

It is important to note that this book provides a comprehensive overview of body piercing, but it is by no means exhaustive. The field of piercing is vast and ever-changing, and there is always more to explore and learn.

In closing, body piercing is an art form that allows individuals to express their unique identity and style. It requires technical skill, professionalism, and a commitment to safety and ethical practices. Whether you are a piercer or someone interested in getting a piercing, we hope that this book has provided valuable insights and knowledge to enhance your understanding and appreciation of this fascinating industry.

Printed in Great Britain
by Amazon

37241088R00076